BUDDIES SHARE THEIR SPIRITUAL JOURNEYS

"In these touching and poignant stories by sixteen men, we encounter a rich exploration of faith. The variety of perspectives is likely to offer readers some narratives that resonate deeply and others that challenge. But all the stories invite reflection on one's own spiritual journey and beliefs."

—BINGHAM POWELL,
rector, St. Mary's Episcopal Church,
Eugene, Oregon

"A group of articulate men consider their lives, their 'spiritual journeys' and essentially tell us how and what brings body and soul into a healthy union. They ask, how important is your early childhood experience of the holy? What's 'religion?' Does church play a role in a healthy journey? What shatters your relationship to the sacred and what are the experiences that knit you into healing and wholeness? Their stories help us notice where and how you become aware of the mysteries of your soul and how you might build a healthy union to your inner life. The men are generous in sharing their experiences with us and their stories offer a compelling invitation to examine our own sacred journeys."

—GERTRUD MUELLER NELSON,
author of *To Dance with God*

"*Buddies* is a well-crafted, moving collection of insights and stories of spiritual journeys shared by members of a men's group led by John Bingham. They discuss the important distinction between the influences of organized religion and the direct spiritual encounters that shaped their lives. John combines his wisdom as an Episcopal Priest and his insights as a psychotherapist to create a unique and very engaging read."

—ALEXANDER SHESTER, MD,
Jungian analyst

"This book is exactly what it says on the cover. It is an account of sixteen male friends getting together to share their spiritual journeys. In an age of toxic masculinity, it is refreshing to read these frank, honest, and emotional stories. They are all very different, because the men come from different backgrounds and have different spiritual experiences. The narrator lets the men speak for themselves, so what we get is an insight into how men think about God."

—MARK HARGREAVES,
rector, St James by-the-Sea,
La Jolla, California

"We live impoverished when disconnected from the individual soundings of the 'Other' in the unvarnished holiness of our friends' lives. John Bingham bridges this gap with a remarkable, connective sharing during a retreat among friends—vulnerably and honestly sharing life stories centered on the holy as individually experienced. The reader is privileged to 'listen in' upon a polyphony of transcendence in these seventeen men's separate journeys, a remarkable blessing that is not to be missed."

—SCOTT STARBUCK,
senior pastor, Manito Presbyterian Church,
Spokane, Washington

Buddies Share Their Spiritual Journeys

Edited by JOHN PRATT BINGHAM

RESOURCE *Publications* · Eugene, Oregon

BUDDIES SHARE THEIR SPIRITUAL JOURNEYS

Resource Publications
An Imprint of Wipf and Stock Publishers
199 W. 8th Ave., Suite 3
Eugene, OR 97401

www.wipfandstock.com

PAPERBACK ISBN: 979-8-3852-3976-4
HARDCOVER ISBN: 979-8-3852-3977-1
EBOOK ISBN: 979-8-3852-3978-8

VERSION NUMBER 03/06/25

Scripture quotations are from the New Revised Standard Version Bible, copyright © 1989 National Council of the Churches of Christ in the United States of America. Used by permission. All rights reserved worldwide.

HUMAN
AUTHORED
AG THE Authors Guild

1419261

To the men who participated in this exercise,
whose stories are reflected in this narrative,
and to James Hubbell,
whose influence touched many lives.

You are not dead yet, it's not too late
to open your depths by plunging into them
and drink in the life
that reveals itself quietly there.

—RAINER MARIA RILKE

CONTENTS

GATHERING

The following pages recount the actual spiritual journeys of seventeen older men, written by them. In editing these stories, I integrated them into a fictitious narrative of an annual retreat. I changed their names as well as key circumstances for anonymity.

On Monday, May 20, 2024, sixteen elderly men and I traveled to a picturesque resort in the heart of Old Town, San Diego. I carefully chose a place that provided comfort and fostered our shared experiences. This was a continuation of a cherished tradition spanning decades that has woven the fabric of our lives together. The setting included a full kitchen and a tuned piano, which brought a smile to Paul's face, our chef and musician extraordinaire. Paul's gourmet meals have been a highlight of our meetings since the early years of tents and campfires. As we shared meals, went on outings, and indulged in snacks, we updated our stories, some of which were true. Our conversations included the hush money trial of Trump, the wars in Gaza and Ukraine, and the implications of Justice Samuel Alito's flying his MAGA flags. These shared experiences, these times of laughter and learning, bind us together.

Since our last meeting, our hearts have been heavy with the loss of two African American members, Ray and Fred. Their energy and humor were a vibrant part of our group, and their absence was keenly felt. Their loss left a void in our discussions and shared experiences. Paul created a floral display in their honor, and Hal brought a painting he'd done of the men. The group observed a moment of silence, a small tribute to their memory and profound impact on our lives. Their empty chairs, once filled with laughter and wisdom, now remind us of our friends' absence.

The passing of Ray and Fred sparked a new direction for our group: to reflect on the deeper aspects of life and the afterlife. We decided to delve into our spiritual journeys, a topic that had never been the group's focus. Initially, the suggestion was met with resistance. It's a challenging subject, especially for those who don't believe a spiritual realm exists. However, after much discussion, we all agreed to share without engaging in theological debates, allowing us to comfortably reveal a deeper, more personal side of ourselves. One member said, "I think the Buddha said something like a candle can't burn without fire and man can't live without a spiritual life." Some toes were stepped on during the presentations, but no one took offense.

I did not define the contents of a spiritual journey for the men, though I did send a list of topics to use as prompts to help them get started. Each fellow chose what to include in his presentation, and their accounts reflect this. What emerged were deeply personal reflections, each a unique soul journey. Sharing this material brought us closer to one another and created intimacy among us.

Our group is a tapestry of diverse backgrounds and experiences, each thread adding richness to our collective journey. We have lawyers, university educators, therapists, priests, blue-collar workers, and a scientist. Quite a few members are veterans, some of whom found solace in their faith after their time in Vietnam. While most identify as Christians, we also have a Jewish member and others who are agnostic or atheist. This diversity was not a source of division but a testament to our unity, respect, and appreciation for each other's paths. Each member feels like he belongs.

The names and identities of this year's participants have been changed to protect their privacy. Their presentations, however, are their actual experiences.

Meet Andy, a Vietnam veteran turned lawyer living in Texas. He stands tall at six-four, has a scraggly beard, and has a penchant for faded T-shirts, shorts, and flip-flops.

Bruce spent over twenty years with the Naval Investigative Service. He likes cigars, beer, and risqué jokes. Bruce is an active member of the American Birding Association, specializing in observing and counting water birds. He lives in California.

George served in the Navy, primarily at the Marine Corps Air Station, Miramar. George wears dark glasses all the time—even indoors. George has had his knees operated on multiple times and walks with a limp. He, too, likes cigars and lives in California.

Hal sold insurance before becoming an Episcopal priest. He enjoys his evening wine, plein air painting, and music from the 1960s. His physical fitness and thick black hair are the envy of the group. He lives in Oregon.

Jim is from New Orleans. He was a college professor before becoming a therapist and author. Jim is bald and has a thick mustache. His hobby is building and selling specialty kites. Jim lives in California.

John is the narrator. I am an Episcopal priest, a licensed therapist, and an author. I have a beard and glasses, love kayaking, and live in California.

Lawrence's career was in finance. He worked in the United States and Europe and enjoys fixing broken electronic devices. Lawrence wears a Stetson hat and western boots and lives on a horse ranch in California.

Mike has a PhD in chemistry and worked for a large corporation on the East Coast and in Europe. He has seven children and twenty-two grandchildren, and the pictures to prove it. Mike loves billiards, has severe scoliosis, and uses a cane. He lives in California.

Paul has a bachelor's degree in anthropology and a Master's in folklore and mythology. He worked professionally in music, the floral industry, and as a baker. His grey hair is shoulder length, often in a ponytail. Paul lives in California.

Peter was a business executive who worked for several well-known corporations. He grew up in New England and loves frisbee golf, pickleball, and lawn bowling. He is short, plump, and a huge college football fan. Peter now lives in California.

Phil was born in Canada. He worked on the radio, for a construction company, and was employed by the United Nations in the Middle East. Phil is our oldest member. He sings in a variety of choirs and reads a book a week. He lives in California.

Richard is a Vietnam veteran who became a lawyer and an executive for a major corporation. He is an active volunteer at his local YMCA and has walked the entire Pacific Rim Trail twice. Richard lives in the state of Washington.

Robert was a Fulbright scholar before receiving his PhD in educational policy. He worked for one of the universities in the Pacific Northwest. Robert is a pilot who enjoys teaching people about gliders and taking them on flights. He lives in Oregon.

Sam was a researcher for the state of California legislature and the Department of Education. He is an environmentalist who spends his retirement tending his garden and volunteering at an animal rescue facility. Sam has grey hair on top of his six-foot-three frame. He lives in California.

Scott worked as a private investigator before receiving his PsyD in psychology. He loves pickleball and has won several tournaments. Scott wears sleeveless shirts and volunteers as a football coach at his local high school. He lives in California.

Steve was a professional golfer before moving into financial management. He operates a nonprofit organization that teaches golf to minority youth. His ready smile lights up the room, and his joke telling keeps everyone laughing. Steve lives in California.

Tim began his career as a pastor before starting an automobile refurbishing company. He has wavy red hair, trophies from his bowling league, and is an avid amateur radio operator. Tim rides a Harley regularly despite his family's objections. Tim lives in California.

Every member had a role in the group's operation, a structure we carefully built over the years. I bought everyone personalized aprons to pay tribute to their contributions. Paul's had Chef on it, while Jim's had Sous Chef. Their aprons were gray with leather straps and a pocket, a uniform they wore proudly.

The cleaning crews received aprons made of water-resistant waxed canvas.

Cleaning Crew A consisted of the men who traveled the farthest. Robert's apron said Captain. The other members of Cleaning Crew A were Andy, Hal, Peter, and Richard. Their aprons were red.

Cleaning Crew B was composed of men from Northern California. Steve was the captain assisted by Phil, Scott, Lawrence, and me. Our aprons were blue.

Cleaning Crew C lived locally. George was the captain. He led Sam, Bruce, Tim, and Mike. Their aprons were bronze.

When we arrived, Paul had warm macadamia cookies and edamame waiting for us. The snacks were next to a sign-up sheet for Tuesday's activities. The men chose from deep-sea fishing, pickleball, a tour of the Midway aircraft carrier, or a visit to the zoo and the Air & Space Museum. Besides the flowers in tribute to Fred and Ray, Paul had bouquets in each room and throughout the common area.

We drew numbers from Larry's Stetson to establish the order of speakers. Peter picked number one. He'd speak first after dinner.

PETER'S JOURNEY
My Higher Power

Paul's dinner consisted of hot wonton soup and orange chicken over fried rice. It was delicious. A round of applause left Paul bowing and grinning.

After the cleaning crew finished, Peter walked to the fireplace hearth, blew out a short breath, looked at the fire, and sat in a wicker chair facing us. The glow from the fire softened the moment. Peter began.

"I grew up in a working-class community. I didn't know anyone who wasn't Roman Catholic. We all went to parochial school; most of my friends and my brother were altar boys. I wanted to be one in the worst way. The nuns told me I was bad, so I wasn't allowed to serve at the altar. I was taught God is to be feared. If I died with a mortal sin, I was going to hell to burn for eternity, no matter how good of a life I may have lived. Purgatory was for those without mortal sins. It was the stopping place to burn for a time to cleanse a lifetime of venial sins. Only when freed of impurities could you be admitted into heaven.

"What really turned me away from the church was the way it treated my father. My mother died when I was two. I had three older siblings. Dad married a lady he didn't love so there would be someone to care for us. The marriage lasted only a year and they divorced. The church, which Dad needed, excommunicated him. Divorce wasn't allowed. Dad was thirty-five years old, had lost his young wife, and had four children to raise. Excommunication wasn't what he needed. It didn't help. He needed the church badly but couldn't partake.

"As I entered my teens, I grew disenchanted with the whole notion of Catholicism and the hocus-pocus of it all. I didn't believe in confession, communion, and the fact of being destined to hell if you died with a mortal sin. However, if you said an 'act of contrition' just before you died, no matter how bad a life you lived, you would go to heaven. What a load of crap." Laughter filled the room.

"I became agnostic until I was in a foxhole in Vietnam. With mortars exploding around me, I said an act of contrition just in case I was wrong." Nervous laughter. "It's true. There really are no atheists in foxholes."

Andy said, "Amen. When it's my turn, I'll tell you about my experience with mortars in Vietnam." A subdued mood permeated the room.

Peter continued.

"As you know, I stepped on a land mine walking back to base camp. Part of my leg was blown away. I thought I was going to die, so I asked the courageous helicopter pilot who rescued me to radio for a priest to give me last rites. The priest didn't show up until the next morning. He asked to hear my confession before proceeding. By then, I knew I wasn't going to die, so I told the priest I didn't believe in confession. He left in a huff.

"The next part of my spiritual journey involved my response to losing my lower leg. I had been an elite athlete in high school. Now, I wasn't. Morphine took away the physical pain, but I needed something for my depression and the demons that told me I was no good. Alcohol did that. I drank virtually every night for over twenty years. I tried to stop but couldn't live without my anesthetic. I checked into an outpatient substance abuse program thirty-four years ago and had a spiritual awakening."

"Tell us about that," said Phil.

"I remember sharing with my recovery group that if I didn't drink, I would never get to sleep. I cried. The other addicts took me in their arms and told me everything was going to be all right. I didn't believe them. The obsession to drink was overpowering. But their support and understanding made a difference. That night, I went home, got into bed with a couple of books, and readied myself for a sleepless night. But I was determined not to drink. After a few minutes of reading, I fell asleep. When I woke the next morning, the obsession to drink was lifted from me. I have never had a desire to drink alcohol since.

"So, what happened? I had no power to quit drinking on my own. A Power greater than myself relieved me of this all-powerful obsession. All I had to do was surrender. It was a moment of profound relief and peace, knowing I was not alone in this struggle.

"Initially, my Higher Power was the recovery group. After a while, I chose Yoda." Low-volume chuckles could be heard. "Hey, Yoda worked for me. Over time, I came to believe in God as I understood him. He lives inside me and will always be there when I need him for guidance. The correct answer is always there if I am open and listen closely to my heart. I use quiet meditation at such moments, especially when I am in pain. God and I walk hand-in-hand. I do this best when I'm in nature. A God of love has replaced the mean God of my youth.

"I want you to know I don't believe in divine intervention. God has a plan for each of us. I don't believe in praying to get God to change his plan. God doesn't tilt the wheel. I don't pray for God to cure my wife of her cancer. I pray he gives me strength and courage to do whatever I can to make her life as enjoyable and peaceful as possible. I also pray for God to relieve me of my most glaring character defects—self-centeredness, laziness, fear, and resentment—so I can be of maximum service to my fellow man. The prayerful part of my journey keeps me motivated and inspired.

"When my wife was first diagnosed with cancer, I thought regular attendance at religious services would help. We sought out services we'd be comfortable attending. We tried different denominations, but none stuck with us. Being spiritual, without a formal religion, works for us. Sports have replaced our need for a religious community. Sports have raised my self-esteem.

"Finally, John asked me to comment on my view of an after-life. For me, there is no life after death. When we die, we are just dead.

"That's the story of my spiritual journey."

(Applause)

* * *

"Let's take a five-minute break," I said.

After the break, I asked, "Who drew number two?"

Mike raised his hand and took Peter's place. Before he began, Mike found a seat cushion that was not being used and settled in.

MIKE'S JOURNEY

A Scientist's Perspective

"I grew up in a village of five thousand people and regularly attended the Methodist church two blocks from home. My father was the church treasurer, and after I left the nest, my mother became the church secretary. I married my high school sweetheart at a young age. We had several children. I worked as an industrial chemist for thirty-four years. My doctoral degree enabled me to travel the world for my employer. That's a quick overview of my life.

"I had a strong belief in God as a child. This continued until I was in my late thirties. It wasn't any single event, at least that I remember, that caused me to start losing my trust in religion. Part of it was the rise of the televangelists, who seemed more interested in raising money than the Golden Rule. Also, I observed mega-churches like the one in Lynchburg, Virginia, appeared to be involved in indoctrination and building a family empire. These behaviors repelled me." "Right on!" was expressed by one of the listeners. Others smiled.

"But there was more to it than that. I started to see religions as a way to explain what was not understood at the time of their founding, as a way for the powerful to control the masses, and as a way for the unscrupulous to exploit others." A nodding of heads could be seen throughout the room.

"A very close friend joined a fundamentalist church. She told us how all the women wore long dresses to the Sunday service. It wasn't required; they just did it. I saw this as the church using peer pressure to enforce conformity. I don't want to step on anyone's toes, but I came to believe that fundamentalist Christians, in effect, believed in a deceitful God. Their belief the Bible is infallible meant God had planted all the evidence of evolution as a way of testing a believer's faith. They were to ignore all the evidence and logic and accept that the universe is only a few thousand years old. This bothered me because it seemed to conflict with my spiritual views. I viewed the Christian God as open and honest, which is my view of the God of the Gospels. I am referring to religions, not faith or spirituality. I stopped practicing a religion.

"That decision created a new question I had to answer: What do I now believe, and how does that affect the way I lead my life? My values and conduct were shaped not by direct teachings but by observing how my parents lived and interacted with others. Three examples stand out from my childhood.

"In the early 1950s, my parents visited my father's World War II buddy. When they returned home, I overheard my parents talking about how appalled they were when Dad's friend proudly told them the community he lived in was *restricted*—that is, no Jews were allowed. My parents also commented on anti-Semitic remarks the fellow and his wife made. These remarks were quietly exchanged between my parents. I just happened to overhear them. I didn't fully understand the meaning for several more years.

"In 1961, my brother came home from college. He told my parents that they did not realize what went on in families: divorce, physical abuse, alcoholism, etc. My parents replied that they knew about those things but chose not to expose their children to them. My parents did not gossip or criticize others, at least not in front of their children.

"In 1962, another brother brought Gene, an Afro-American college friend, home for the weekend. It was Gene's birthday. My mother baked him a cake, and we thought nothing of it. It was just how we were expected to treat all people. Gene stayed in touch with my parents for years.

"I became aware of the following after I was married. My parents would learn there was a family in need of food. They would gather bags of nonperishable food and leave them on the doorstep. My sister asked why my mother didn't ring the doorbell. Mother replied that the families were proud and would refuse charity. Leaving the food as we did, they had to accept it. My parents did not seek credit for the good they did but derived satisfaction from helping others. This amazes me more when I think my parents had six children, and my father was an hourly shift worker. There was little to spare, but what they had, they shared with others.

"As an adult, I realized my parents were viewed as trustworthy and scrupulously honest. Their integrity was a source of admiration for me and those who knew them. My father was the church treasurer for decades, as well as treasurer for the fire company, bowling league, and his carpool to work. People knew my mother would not gossip and that what she learned as church secretary would never be revealed.

"Now I realize the example my parents set has significantly influenced my life. They did it by their deeds. They 'walked the talk.' I try to conduct my life as my parents did theirs. I've been a scout leader, a volunteer fireman, and a hiking trail maintenance volunteer. I assist older people on mid-week hikes and walk their dogs when they cannot. I donate significantly to charities that focus on education, recreation, and animal welfare. I look out for those around me and willingly assist others whenever possible.

"As I became troubled by what I observed about religions, I started to evolve toward being an agnostic and then toward being a questioning atheist. My spirituality declined and slowly disappeared. I lost faith in a god. An honest atheist scientist is as bothered by what we don't understand as a deeply spiritual individual. We both seek to learn the how and why of the universe. A spiritual human seeks through faith and belief that this is not all there is. An atheist scientist also seeks truth but struggles to accept the current laws and theories because, as an honest person, so little is understood.

"As an atheist scientist, I wonder if today's science will be looked back upon in one hundred years as laughable, just as we look back on previous centuries' beliefs that we now believe to be wrong. The 'standard model' of physics, quantum mechanics, and general relativity 'explains' a portion of what we observe, but just a portion.

"At times, I am as uncomfortable being an atheist as I would be as a spiritual person. How can we rule out a greater being when we know so little? But if there is a superior being, in what way is this revealed? Nearly all the explanations of the past have proven to be natural phenomena. I would like to believe in a benevolent god, but I see so much evil and suffering that if there is a god, I don't feel the god's presence. I know many good people, but they are just naturally good. They are offset by the people who seem naturally cruel, deceiving liars. Our experiences and what we observed as children and adolescents shaped us. You are what you are because of where you were when.

"I don't believe in an afterlife. But then, I evaluate my actions and operational values and ask what I learned. I talk to my late wife and visit my parents' graves regularly. Is this a form of prayer, or does it mean respect for those I have loved? Is it an unconscious belief in an afterlife of some type? Am I just trying to summon into consciousness the wisdom and guidance I received from them in the past? I find myself challenged to formulate a set of beliefs, or nonbeliefs, on a solid foundation.

"There is a Buddhist parable about a disciple of a religion who tries to convert the Buddha to his faith. The Buddha replies that no one can know with certainty about an afterlife or a god. Therefore, all beliefs are equally valid—people forget that Buddhism is a philosophy, not a religion.

"I want to know if there is an afterlife, but that is impossible. Certainty about these things cannot be fact based. The negative proof is impossible. So, what can I do? How do I come to my personal beliefs? What do I hold to be true? And how do I reconcile the necessary uncertainty?

"I have said I do not believe in an afterlife and that I am an atheist. This is mainly driven by a sense that we are each a unique collection of chemical elements assembled by a natural process into sentient beings. From my vantage point, there is nothing special about us. We are not 'God's Chosen.' Other species on this planet each possess some but not all the characteristics we think make us unique. Time and chance events have allowed evolution to shape us to benefit from our environment. This results in convergent evolution, e.g., the marsupial wolf of Australia and the leopard seals of the Antarctic filling the same ecological niche as polar bears in the Arctic.

"Expanding on this belief, it is doubtful that we are the only sentient beings in the universe. They probably do not look like us. If they have DNA, it may be right-handed rather than left-handed as ours is, making them our mirror image. They may be primitive, as we were ten thousand years ago. Or the planet they will live on may still need to have a chance event to create an environment that can allow them to evolve. Or they may have destroyed themselves. All these and more scenarios exist in the observable universe.

"However, I firmly believe that they will, in many ways, mirror our cultural and intellectual development. As I have traveled, I have marveled at the similarities of cultures that were isolated from each other. A wall at Angkor Wat and one at Tikal look identical because they had access to the same resources. The same comparison is accurate for Egypt and the Inca.

"The Fermi paradox is, since extraterrestrial life almost certainly exists, why haven't they contacted us? While it's enjoyable to speculate, e.g., the zoo hypothesis, sentient beings are too far away. How would they know where to look? The assumption that is being made is that according to the current laws of physics, you cannot travel or communicate faster than the speed of light. Maybe these 'laws' are not true. We see hints that communication can be faster than the speed of light in the correlation of specific sets of subatomic particles. Scientists need to be humble regarding their beliefs because we know so little. After learning about a new class of subatomic particles, the Nobel Prize-winning American physicist I. I. Rabi famously said, 'Who ordered that?' Indeed, all humans need to be humble concerning their beliefs.

"I will summarize my ramblings:

1. I was very religious as a youth.

2. Sometime in my thirties, I began to lose my faith as I observed how religion is often used to manipulate and control people and to aggrandize religious leaders.

3. I came to view religion as a net negative in the world.

4. The more critically I observed the world, the more my spirituality declined.

5. I came to view humanity as a natural product of the universe, not unique.

6. I stopped believing in the existence of a higher being and an afterlife.

7. After self-examination, I realized my beliefs are no more valid than those who believe in a higher being and an afterlife.

8. I tolerate others' beliefs except when they accept their beliefs without question.

9. I conduct my life based on the values I obtained from watching how my parents conducted their lives.

"Finally, I want to share two experiences that challenge what I have come to believe.

"The first is a friend's experience. In high school, my friend's father was in the hospital dying while my friend was trying out for the school baseball team. When he visited his father for the last time, his father asked how the tryout went.

"'I am going to be the shortstop,' my friend replied.

"After his father died, my friend deeply regretted that the last thing he said to his father was a lie. He didn't know if he made the team, much less what position he'd play. When he returned to school after the funeral, the coach announced he would be the shortstop. This made my friend's last words true and removed his burden.

"My friend never has been active in a church, but he is spiritual. He believes God acts through people, such as the coach, to ease people's pain. My friend is a significant donor to and supporter of recreation activities in the town where we grew up.

"The other experience was my sister's. She was an identical twin when she was born, but her twin died during the birth. This was in the fifties before ultrasounds. My parents weren't expecting twins.

"When my sister was in kindergarten, she ran across the street to wait for the school bus, which had just come into sight. I saw her get hit by a car, go up onto the hood of the car, and then, as the car braked, fly off the hood and bounce down the street. The driver was a family friend who had no way to avoid hitting my sister.

"My sister was bruised and scraped but unharmed. When asked what happened, my sister said she was not hit. The 'other little girl was hit.' My sister said she watched the accident from sitting in the elm tree in our front yard. My sister recently told me that her twin, her guardian angel, came from heaven, placed her safely in the tree, and took the impact for her. Then, her twin placed her back onto the road. To this day, my sister has an unshakable faith. She is very active in her parish, devoting weeks to parish projects. She believes her twin is always watching over her, and she wants her ashes to be placed on her twin's grave when she dies."

"I believe in guardian angels," said George. "I'll tell you about mine when it's my turn."

"I'll look forward to it," replied Mike. "I'll stop here as this is where my path has led me. Thank you for listening."

(Applause)

* * *

"Let's take a fifteen-minute break," I said. "Paul has refreshments for us."

"Vanilla ice cream is on the counter," said Paul. "Use the various toppings to make yourself a sundae."

"We have time for two more presentations tonight," I announced. "Who drew number three?"

"I did," said Steve, applying slices of fresh strawberries and whipped cream to his bowl.

STEVE'S JOURNEY
Spirituality Is in My DNA

"My spiritual path has taken me on a fascinating journey. I am one of those guys who pursued subjects in college that I haven't used in my professional life. I majored in English literature and political science. Yet, I've spent most of my life on a golf course or managing other people's money. These seemingly unrelated careers have taught me valuable lessons about integrity, responsibility, and accountability, which are integral to my spiritual journey. For instance, in golf, I learned the importance of personal discipline and perseverance, which have been instrumental in my spiritual growth. In money management, I learned about the ethical use of resources and the impact of our financial decisions on others.

"I grew up in a small Episcopal church in Northern California. Around the age of five, I attended Sunday school and services. By eight, I was an acolyte."

"What's that?" asked George.

"An acolyte is an altar boy. I served the priest and congregation until I was fifteen, when we moved. At our new home, I played golf instead of going to church. Today, I'll occasionally go to a Sunday service, usually of the Episcopal or Catholic variety.

"My college years were a spiritual turning point. As an All-American golfer and Christian, I was a prime target for my campus's Fellowship of Christian Athletes. The Fellowship's approach to Christianity did not align with mine. Their aggressive recruitment and tribalism put me off, as did their dogmatism, which was in stark contrast to my private, evolving beliefs. My beliefs, shaped by my experiences and personal reflection, are more open minded and inclusive, focusing on love, compassion, and personal growth. Realizing this marked a moment of significant self-discovery. It allowed me to continue my journey in my way, which has been slow but steady, punctuated by moments of enlightenment.

"Do I believe in a Higher Power? Absolutely! Is it God or humanity as a whole? The verdict is still out for me. I embrace the unknown as an exciting and integral part of the journey, a space where curiosity and openness thrive.

"John asked us to think about how we express our beliefs. I do that by interacting with the people in my life. I have an inner code that I adhere to in all that I do. Spirituality is in my DNA."

"How do you nurture yourself spiritually?" asked Hal.

"Good question. I nurture myself primarily in three ways. I engage in daily meditation, which aids in quieting my mind, focusing my thoughts, and connecting with my inner self. This practice has been instrumental in my spiritual journey, helping me to find inner peace and clarity amidst life's challenges.

"I also immerse myself in my love of reading, which has been a constant companion since I was a lad. I devour several books monthly, finding wisdom and inspiration in diverse spiritual and secular texts. Reading has continually refreshed my soul, broadened my perspective, and deepened my understanding of the world and my place in it.

"The third way I renew myself is by being with my wife, children, and grandchildren. They are a wellspring of immense joy that constantly reminds me of the importance of love, connection, and family in my spiritual journey. I thank God for them. I always seek other avenues to nurture myself and enrich my journey, such as engaging in meaningful conversations, exploring nature, and practicing gratitude.

"Death, surprisingly enough, doesn't frighten me. Do I hope there is something after? Of course. Either way, I am at peace with whatever comes. I feel blessed with the extraordinary years I have lived already. Each day is a gift, and I am grateful for the experiences and lessons they have brought. Do I want another fifteen to twenty years? Absolutely! I have more to do, more to learn, and more to share!

"I don't have stories or experiences like Mike and Peter, but I have my path and am curious about where it leads. This curiosity, fueled by my desire for personal growth and spiritual enlightenment, propels my journey and motivates me to explore new horizons, as I am being exposed to in my conversations with you.

"I am evolving, constantly learning, and growing. I am a work in progress on a journey far from over."

(Applause)

* * *

"Let's take a five-minute break," I said. "Who drew number four?"

Andy raised his hand. He slipped on his flip-flops and moved next to the fire.

ANDY'S JOURNEY
Committed to Christ

"I was close to my father. He supported me in everything I did. He came to all my high school football games and wrestling matches. He encouraged me to go to law school when I returned from Vietnam and supported me when I became a deputy district attorney. I loved my dad.

"I grew up in Southern California. Though my parents considered themselves Christians, we rarely attended church except on Easter. I knew Jesus Christ lived two thousand years ago and died on a cross. Still, I did not understand what having a personal relationship with him meant. By the time I reached college, the only things that interested me were parties, beer, and girls.

"When I went to college, I stopped attending church and didn't return until I came home from Vietnam. I drank a lot of beer in college and the Army. I witnessed a lot of career soldiers who became alcoholics, and that caused me to reduce significantly my consumption when I got back from overseas."

"Good thinking," said Peter. "I wish I had."

"In 1968, after I graduated from college, I received orders to go to Vietnam as a Second Lieutenant in the United States Army. I was assigned to a combat engineer battalion stationed in Pleiku in the Central Highlands near the Cambodian border. When I arrived, another young lieutenant had almost completed his tour of duty, and it was my job to take his place. He had only one week left before he was going home. During that week, he and I drove to various job sites so that he could familiarize me with the duties I'd assume. One day, he was following me when his jeep hit a mine. He was killed. I became furious at a God I didn't know. I should have been killed, not him. He had completed his year in Vietnam. He had a wife and two young children waiting for him. I was single.

"Our battalion received orders to move south to Bam Me Thout a month later. The night before we were to leave, the Vietcong started shelling our base camp with mortar rounds. We were sleeping in tents, and suddenly, the first round came in, the second, and then the third. I heard a round hit right next to our tent, and then I waited for the next one to hit us, but it never came. Then, one exploded on the other side of us, and the rounds began to move farther and farther away. When the shelling finally stopped, we found that the tent next to us had taken a direct hit. One soldier had been killed, and the other seven men were critically wounded. They had to be flown to Japan. When the sun came up, we discovered a trailer full of explosives had been mistakenly parked right outside our tent. The mortar round I had been waiting for landed in the middle of that trailer and failed to explode. If it had gone off, there was enough dynamite and C-4 to blow up everybody within fifty feet. I was only ten feet away.

"There were other incidents during that year: night attacks where 122 mm rockets whistled in on top of us, other mortar attacks, going out on night patrols, and running convoys along jungle roads where ambushes were common. But God protected me, and I left Vietnam not knowing him but believing that maybe there was a God and he had a plan for my life.

"In Vietnam, everybody had their god. For some, it was their girlfriend or their wife who wrote them every week. However, I knew that human relationships could not replace God. Sometimes, these soldiers received Dear John letters telling them their wives or girlfriends had been unfaithful. One of the guys in our unit received one of these letters and blew his brains out. Other young soldiers dreamed about new cars, stereo equipment, or upscale cameras. I knew that material possessions would never give meaning to my life.

"When I returned to California, I started attending a Bible study in the home of some Christians. I wanted to intellectually determine whether the Bible was true and whether there was a God. After five months of studying the Bible, I was convinced everything written in it was true. On January 1, 1970, I asked Jesus Christ to come into my heart, and I felt him enter in a very real and personal way. He has been with me ever since.

"After committing to Christ, my family and I attend church every Sunday and Wednesday night. I am also part of our church's prison ministry team. Every Tuesday night, we go to a women's prison and teach Bible study to forty to sixty women for two hours. I attended Bible college at night for two years after law school.

"I believe in prayer and have seen people healed through prayer."

"As have I," said Hal.

"I am not afraid of death. I believe I have the promise of eternal life through Jesus Christ's death on the cross. Among the many Scriptures that are the foundation of my faith, Rom 5:8 says it as well as any: 'God proves his love for us in that while we were still sinners, Christ died for us.' John 3:16 says, 'For God so loved the world that he gave his only Son so that everyone who believes in him may not perish but may have eternal life.'

"Other verses that form the foundation of my faith are John 14:6; Rom 3:23, 6:23, and 10:9; Heb 9:22; 1 Pet 3:18; and 1 John 1:9. I hope you will read, learn, and inwardly digest them.

"I'll close with Rev 3:20, which captures my experience, so I know it is true. It says, 'Listen! I am standing at the door, knocking; if you hear my voice and open the door, I will come into you and eat with you, and you with me.'"

(Applause)

* * *

"This is a good stopping point for the night, though after hearing about Andy's experiences in Vietnam, I doubt I'll be able to sleep for a while," I said.

"Person five will start tomorrow. Who picked number five?"

Phil replied, "That would be me."

"No sleeping in tomorrow. The outings will begin right after breakfast clean-up."

PHIL'S JOURNEY
A Spirituality of Imperfection

On our first full day, breakfast consisted of bananas, scrambled eggs, warm cinnamon rolls, bacon, granola, and raisins. Coffee was in abundant supply, though tea was also available.

Paul had sandwiches ready for us to take on our various outings. We could have turkey, ham, or tuna on wheat or sourdough. Potato chips and apples were part of our lunch bags.

When we returned from our adventures, chocolate chip and oatmeal raisin cookies awaited us. Most of us took some of each.

Dinner was bouillabaisse. The rockfish and sea bass our fishermen brought back were incorporated into it. Jim made a salad that included asparagus, avocados, and red onion with a poppy seed, ranch, or blue cheese dressing. Slices of baguettes were on the tables. We ate well.

After cleaning up, Phil, our oldest member, took his turn.

"The trip to the zoo was fun, but the visit to the Air & Space Museum was thrilling. Learning about the history of flying, from its beginnings in 1783 with the first hot-air balloon to today's complicated aircraft, was new to me. I liked the section dedicated to space travel the most. Viewing space suits and the Apollo 9 command module stimulated my imagination. I was there with them, testing the lunar module for the first time in space. Those astronauts were incredibly courageous.

"I grew up on a farm in central Canada, where I could see the fullness of the night sky. As a boy, I often fantasized about traveling among the stars and even landing on the moon. Apollo 9's mission brought my little boy's fantasies closer to reality, and I appreciated them for it.

"Turning to my spiritual journey, I was raised as a Roman Catholic, which introduced me to a God of somebody else's conception. That God was a formidable personage, like the one I heard about in the Bible. He *watched and noted* my every move, particularly the 'bad' ones. As I grew, I developed reservations about my soul being an *object* monitored by a personage.

"Offsetting this image of a judgmental God was the influence of my parents. They repeated the dogmas/rules we heard in church, but I saw their loving behavior. Like Mike, my parents became the focus of my life. I witnessed their actions, informed by principles/values like honesty, forgiveness, helpfulness, truth, and clean living. Work ethics like diligence and compassion were priorities. That was enough for me to be less concerned about the personage taking notes.

"When I was young, I found describing spirituality difficult or impossible. I had no words, just actions, and I tried to imitate my parents' loving behavior. The only advice my parents offered me was to listen to my conscience. That was mysterious but okay.

"The entire family prayed together every evening, particularly in winter when adults did not have to be in the fields. These prayers, like the long rosary, did not please my older brothers, who were unhappy about it. I didn't mind. I liked the repetitions, which reminded me of a mantra.

"Then, a shock.

"I was sent to a boarding school run by a religious order *in the city!* I hated being in the city. I missed the farm and the night sky, and I missed my mom, who died the same year. I was thirteen.

"One memory I have pertains to the beginning of each school year. The nuns would bring in a hired preacher-priest to lead a retreat. He told us nothing but scary stories. An example is an account he presented as a real story. A boy supposedly was walking to the village church to confess he'd masturbated. On the way, the boy was hit by a truck and killed.

"'Now,' the priest said, 'the boy is in hell because he was unable to reach the confessional.'

"This story left a lasting impression on me because it exemplified a fear-based spirituality, a stark contrast to the love-based spirituality I had witnessed in my parents. Instead of instilling fear in me and my peers, the priest's story highlighted the stark contrast between fear and love in spirituality. We had no words for our perception, just a growing awareness.

"Later, I was surprised to find a natural educator at a college run by the same order. He was brilliant, thoughtful, and respectful. His approach to spirituality was based on personal perception, not just what was preached in church. I was inspired by his perspective. It significantly shaped my new understanding of spirituality.

"During my college years, I worked part time as a radio announcer and commercial writer. I was passionate about this work and considered pursuing a radio, television, and communications career. However, upon graduation, I entered seminary to explore becoming a priest, like one of my brothers. The canon law classes I took cast doubt that becoming a priest was right for me. While I embraced the logic and ethics of Thomas Aquinas, I also appreciated that reality is both what you see and the awareness of what you do not see. Later in life, I realized my awareness of the unseen was a love of mystery: there are no firm final answers.

"I left the seminary after one session: September to December."

"I wish I had," said Jim, shaking his head.

"My radio manager offered me a full-time job. I accepted and prepared to begin in early January. The bishop I would have reported to if I had become a priest asked to meet with me during the Christmas period. He told me why I was making a mistake, then said he had spoken to the radio station manager. My job had been canceled, though I had yet to hear this from the station manager. The bishop had lots of reasons why the cancellation was good for me.

"This incident didn't nullify my religious-based spirituality, but it put a big dent in it. If this happened today, I might sue the man. Many years later, I understood that spirituality involves learning to live with imperfection. The bishop was wrong and imperfect. This realization allowed me to forgive him.

"My life changed, but I held on to the past. I got a job on a large hydraulic construction site. I hated it when my coworkers said I looked like a priest. I still had my black briefcase and a coat you don't bring to a construction site. I continued to attend church functions, but I became aware that the church's beliefs (like not having sex before marriage) were making my life difficult. I wished I didn't have a conscience!"

"Isn't that the truth!" said George. Chuckles spread across the room.

"My spirituality at this time was driven by a rules-based past rather than by who I was spiritually. The rules I followed were important, but I needed to learn the difference.

"I was transferred to the company headquarters, where I met and married a Catholic lady with whom I practiced the rituals of religion. We rarely talked about our spiritual selves. I now realize that using words to define spirituality is as challenging as coming up with words when I suddenly come across a wild rose.

"I entered a prestigious university and obtained a master's degree in the science of organizational dynamics/development. The degree opened opportunities for me. I worked for the United Nations in Gaza for two-and-a-half years while my family lived in Canada. Working in Gaza taught me something was wrong with the world; however, amid this darkness, my parents' enduring values resurfaced. *My* spirituality emerged through genuine service to refugees.

"When I returned to Canada, my wife and I raised a family. I got very involved in 'my job.' 'My job' was to have a job and be a provider. In Gaza, I began drinking to relieve my frustration with the world's imperfections. Indeed, alcohol became more and more the answer. I put God on the back burner and developed self-sufficiency. Bad news.

"I joined AA. When I read *The Big Book*, I found this message in the chapter "We Agnostics":

> Deep down in every man, woman, and child is the fun-
> damental idea of God. It may have been obscured by
> calamity, pomp, by the worship of other things, but in
> some form or other, it is there.[1]

"That passage was huge for me. I had somehow lost my soul while worshipping other things like jobs, money, sex, and reputation. Working on my fifth step, I had a profound experience of guilt. I shared this with a monk, who gave me the gift of forgiveness. He said, 'Don't you think God has forgiven you for your past deeds and omissions by now? If not, pray for the gift of faith.'

"Freed from my past guilt, I strongly desired to seek God more consciously. I worked on my self-awareness. I learned to accept myself as an angel or a beast. My spirituality became increasingly based on the acceptance of myself.

"I now see myself as a spirit in the vast, mysterious universe. I have faith in a Power beyond me. I am no longer trapped in self-reliance. I now ask my spirit for quiet and get an awareness of the wonderful mystery of my life and the universe. I don't have all the answers, which is part of my spiritual awareness. My conception of God is the acceptance of a mystery. I don't know what God is and do not need to *know*. For every answer I have to describe God, there is always another question.

"Recently, a friend of sixty years and business partner was preparing for his death. Being curious, he was reading a lot of after-life literature. He asked me what my thoughts were. I told him this story.

"My mother passed away in 1947, and my dad in 1965. Every morning, shortly after waking, I spend quiet time with a daily reader. As I open the book, I meet my Mom and Dad via a picture on their funeral cards, which I have saved for over fifty years. I greet them and thank them daily for being significant contributors to bringing me to life. In joyful gratitude, I acknowledge their nonphysical presence and move on with my day. This is my sense of the *after*, which spirit-wise never ceases to be present . . . if I stay

---

1. *Alcoholics Anonymous*, 55.

aware and bonded. I told my friend, 'It will be the same for you! This is the beautiful mystery of spirituality!'

"My friend was silent on the phone for a good while. Then he said, 'Thank you. I sometimes forget about the nonphysical presence of many people I love; now I can return to this mystery.'

"Step eleven of the AA recovery program is vital to me. It says:

> Sought through prayer and meditation to improve our conscious contact with God *as we understood Him*, praying only for knowledge of His will for us and the power to carry that out.[2]

"That step reminds me to seek contact regularly. Prayer, particularly thanksgiving prayers, is part of my daily life, more so than petition prayers. Gratitude and thanksgiving spiritually feed me as I go through my day.

"Conscious contact does not necessarily mean I will have thoughts or feelings about that contact. Awareness, to me, is a state of 'being.' Words and understanding come later if I am willing and able to be in harmony with a Power greater than me . . . and within me.

"Since I may not have found the exact vocabulary to describe my spirituality and my journey toward it, I will paraphrase from the book *The Spirituality of Imperfection*:

> To have an answer to the question of what spirituality is is to have misunderstood the question. Truth, wisdom, goodness, and beauty resemble spirituality because they are intangible, ineffable realities. We may know them, but can never grasp them with our hands or words. These entities have neither color nor texture; they can't be gauged in inches, ounces, or degrees; they do not make a noise to be measured in decibels; they have no distinct feel as do silk, wood, or cement; they give no odor, they have no taste, they occupy no space. And yet, they exist; they are.[3]

---

2. *Alcoholics Anonymous*, 59.

3. Kurtz and Ketcham, *Spirituality of Imperfection*, 15.

A spirituality of imperfection suggests that spirituality's first step involves facing oneself squarely, seeing oneself as one is: mixed-up, paradoxical, incomplete, and imperfect. Flawedness is the first fact about human beings. Paradoxically, in that imperfect foundation, we find not despair but joy. Only within the reality of our imperfection can we find the peace and serenity we crave.[4]

Spirituality is, above all, a way of life. We don't just think about, feel, or sense it around us. We live it. Spirituality permeates the core of our human be-ing, affecting how we perceive the world around us, how we feel about that world, and the choices we make based on our perceptions and sensations. In the experience of spirituality, three essential elements are always at play: what we see, how we feel, and why we choose.[5]

"Thanks to Ernest Kurtz and Katherine Ketcham for helping me find some powerful words."

(Applause)

＊ ＊ ＊

"We'll take a five-minute break," I said.

4. Kurtz and Ketcham, *Spirituality of Imperfection*, 20.
5. Kurtz and Ketcham, *Spirituality of Imperfection*, 68.

GEORGE'S JOURNEY

*Relying on My Guardian Angel
and Saint Jude*

"I went to the Midway Museum, which is the carrier itself. Having spent most of my professional life with top-gun pilots on land, I was interested in learning about life on an aircraft carrier.

"The first thing that caught my eye was the one hundred loaves of bread needed daily to feed the crew. Yet the 10,500 cups of coffee the crew consumed every day is what boggled my mind. Can you imagine brewing coffee day and night for that many users? Some of the crew must do nothing but brew coffee.

"The highlight of today's visit was taking a combat ride in an F-18 via a simulator. I was launched off the flight deck, and I controlled the plane. I could make it roll, spin, somersault, and loop during my engagement with the enemy. I tried to stay calm as conditions changed and I was learning to fly. I failed to hit most targets before the mission ended, but at least I got a few! There is so much to see and do on the Midway that I will be going back.

"I want to begin sharing my thoughts on my spiritual journey by thanking John. The opportunity to reflect on my spirituality energized me. I probably wouldn't have done the exercise without his encouragement. So, thank you."

I smiled and gave George a thumbs-up.

"Like many of you, my spiritual journey was shaped by my family. I was raised in a loving, nurturing New York Irish Catholic family—like everyone on my street was. You knew you were part of the same tribe when you walked into a stranger's house and saw the same two pictures in the entryway: The Sacred Heart of Jesus and a photo of JFK." Chuckles.

"My parents were devout Roman Catholics and lived what they preached. My father never went to bed without getting down on his knees and saying the rosary. I'm not that devout.

"I was the lucky recipient of eight years of Catholic grammar school (nuns), four years of Catholic high school (brothers), and one year of Saint John's University. I could have been a better student. I got by because of an uncanny ability to score well on multiple-choice tests and a combination of my Guardian Angel and Saint Jude, who have been guiding me through life's challenges and providing me with strength and resilience.

"My Guardian Angel has been a steadfast companion, watching over and protecting me for seventy-six years. I cherish having a brief conversation with him whenever I want. Yes, he's a male. Usually, a simple 'thank you' to him brings me immense comfort and gratitude. I was introduced to my Guardian Angel by Gramma. As the only boy on both sides of the family, I had a reputation for being a real handful."

"They got that right," shouted Peter. "Is that why you always wear dark glasses? So the authorities won't recognize you?"

Laughter filled the room. With a wide grin, George gave Peter the finger and said, "See if I ever show you mercy on the pickleball court again. You're lucky I chose to go to the Midway instead of humiliating you on the court.

"My gramma used to advise me that since I was always getting into trouble, I should maintain a good relationship with my Guardian Angel. And so, I did. He has been there for me in countless ways, big and small. I remember when he helped me find my lost baseball mitt when I was about to give up hope. That's a small but significant instance of his intervention in my life."

"He's hidden your hair," bellowed Tim, laughing so hard he could hardly talk. "Ask him for it back. You've got to do something to cover that head of yours. The light bounces off it and blinds me when we play pickleball."

George, grinning broadly, put his hands on his hips and said to Tim, "You just wish you had as attractive a head as I have. Come on, guys, let me talk.

"I was the only guy with a Saint Jude statue on his dresser. It was a gift from Gramma. She gave it to me because he is the saint of impossible causes. The statue still has a place of honor on my dresser. I save my prayers to Saint Jude for the big stuff. Regrettably, several 'big stuff' events have happened, especially in my younger days. Premature death or Leavenworth was not out of the question on at least one occasion. The details are private. I haven't shared them with anyone, and I'm not ready to do so now. I ask you to trust me when I say Saint Jude has been there for me every time, a beacon of hope in the darkest of times.

"I'm a data-driven guy, not a big believer in coincidence. But I have had too many incidences where a prayer to Saint Jude or a conversation with my Angel has made all the difference. I'm a believer.

"I have gone through phases in my life where I was not a 'good' Catholic and was more of a CEO. I stayed away from church because I thought I didn't need it. Eventually, I was humbled and returned to the flock.

"I enjoy going to Mass, especially now in my later years. What drives me to skip Mass is the lack of the priest's or deacon's ability to deliver a decent homily. It is not just my home church. I also see it when I attend elsewhere. I've worked to get one of my daughters to start attending Mass again. I'm embarrassed by how poorly the clergy speak and how unprepared they are when she comes with us. Reading an article copied from the *Pastoral Review* rather than looking you in the eye or speaking extemporaneously isn't inspiring. My daughter visits an evangelical service and calls me to tell me how uplifting the service is. It pains me that the laity can't hire and fire. We pay the church and the diocese to develop the clergy.

There must be improvement in the training of deacons and priests because the current ways aren't working. It's disheartening to see the church uninspiring.

"The part of the Mass I enjoy most is getting on my knees and conversing with God before the service starts. That's the best.

"I hold a firm belief in eternity and heaven. My God is a God of love and forgiveness, a belief that fills me with hope and the assurance that I'll be reunited with my family in heaven, who are waiting for me. Gramma will introduce me to Saint Jude and my Guardian Angel. My belief in the afterlife brings me comfort and a sense of peace, and I hope it can do the same for you."

(Applause)

* * *

"After another five-minute break, number seven is up. Who is that?" I asked.

Hal indicated he drew number seven.

HAL'S JOURNEY
An Intentional Christian Quest

"Like Phil, I went to the zoo and the Air & Space Museum. Unlike Phil, I got more out of the zoo than the Air & Space Museum. Being in nature is one of the things I love to do, and the San Diego Zoo is as much a botanical garden as it is a keeper of animals. There are something like seven hundred thousand exotic plants on the grounds. There is an African rainforest for the gorillas, a snow forest like the one that covers most of Canada, Alaska, and Russia, and an Arctic tundra for the polar bears. There are aviaries in which birds fly free. How exciting is that! The San Diego Zoo is truly a special place, representing all parts of the world. It feeds my soul. I love it."

"I had no idea there were that many exotic plants there," said Steve. "They must have master gardeners because I kill every plant I get close to."

"You're not alone in having that skill, Steve," said Richard. "The only things I kill faster than plants are goldfish."

Chuckles spread across the room. When the laughter subsided, Hal continued.

"My belief system, which may differ from many of yours, is a testament to the transformative power of a spiritual journey. Let me share how I found the faith that now guides my life.

"My education: I have a bachelor of music therapy, a master of divinity, and a life underwriter degree for the insurance work I once did.

"When I was a senior in high school, I was in a bizarre car accident. I had just dropped my mother off at choir practice when an unknown car abruptly pulled in front of me, revved it in reverse, and slammed into my VW Bug at a staggering forty miles an hour. He went over the top of my car, smashing the windows and the roof, then left. While my car was totaled, I was completely unhurt. I wasn't even cut by flying glass. This bizarre incident made the front page of two Bay Area newspapers, including a photo of me standing next to my demolished car!

"The car accident got me thinking, 'Why wasn't I hurt?' This incident stimulated my spiritual search, leading me to dive deeper into my faith.

"Three months later, I was hitchhiking across Europe for the summer. I was reading a small, complete, leather-bound Old and New Testament that my evangelical girlfriend had given me for the trip. I read the Bible from the back to the front, which was my habit then. I didn't have the patience to find out how a story would end. I had no idea how the Bible was organized.

"However, when I got to the Acts of the Apostles and the Gospel of John, I realized that the person of Jesus was the same person I have known interiorly all my life. As a child, because of the dysfunction of my family and the mental illness and abuse from my mother, along with the absence of my work-related-traveling father, I spent as much time as possible outdoors in the countryside. I climbed trees, explored creeks, and had my favorite sitting rocks, where I would ponder things alone for hours. In the safety of nature, I experienced a strong sense of God's love and presence as far back as I can remember. I found that the Jesus of the Gospels was the person I have always known personally. Now, I knew the person's name. Thus began my intentional Christian journey.

"I want to share two stories. Both occurred while I was on my European trip. The first took place while I was in England. I camped in a wheat field alongside the road to Dover. It was during the 1971 summer solstice. While late, there was still some light, though whatever sunlight remained was blocked by swirling clouds. My friend I was traveling with fell asleep immediately. I lay on my back in my sleeping bag, lost in thought, most likely a form of prayer. Then, unexpectedly, a cloud formed a distinct circle directly above me. Light came from behind the cloud. This continued for at least one minute and got my full attention. As I gazed at the circle of light above me, it changed into a man, his head and upper shoulders.

"The image continued for at least two more minutes. Then, the clouds moved and filled in the circle of light, and it disappeared. I was amazed. The circle of light appeared for a second time before forming the image of a man in a long robe down to his ankles. His arms were outstretched, and the palms of his hands were quite visible in outline. This image remained steady for at least two minutes before merging with the other clouds.

"This experience deeply moved me. In my quiet conversations with God during the next few days, I asked if the images I saw were Jesus. The intuitive answer I received was affirmative. I felt reassured that I had witnessed a vision or trace of a spiritual dimension. The Jesus of the Gospels revealed himself to me this way and through reading the New Testament. I asked my companion if he had seen the same vision, but he was asleep and had no recollection of the event. I was alone in the experience.

"While I understood that the vision I witnessed was unnecessary for my fledging faith in the risen Christ, it affirmed me interiorly. Ever since, I have held on to this experience with thanksgiving.

"The second story occurred when I stayed in a one-thousand-bed youth hostel in Zurich. I read a tract from the literature table that straightforwardly explained that God's nature was like two sides of a coin: one side was love, and the other was justice. The tract said that Jesus was crucified to make my relationship with God whole and remove all obstacles to God. That made sense. I began to pray *through* Jesus. This experience strengthened my sense of God's presence.

"During my stay at the Zurich hostel, I encountered a fellow traveler suffering from dysentery. I visited him that night. His condition was severe, and he was in a lot of pain. Several young men offered him advice and street drugs, but I knew that what he needed wasn't a quick fix but a miracle. I spoke out loud and clear, declaring that I had just prayed to Jesus for the man's healing and that he would be entirely well by 8 a.m. As I spoke, I felt a deep sense of joy and wonder, a confirmation of the power of faith and prayer, much to the surprise and even anger of the others present.

"The following day, we gathered around the man. Someone shook him awake. He sat up, held his face in his hands, and exclaimed loudly, 'Holy shit, my fever's gone!' This was my first experience of healing prayer through Jesus. And there would be many more. The sense of awe and wonder I felt at that moment was indescribable. Andy knows what I am talking about."

"I do, brother Hal," Andy said.

"These incidents made a deep impression on me. Returning home, I went to college. I attended InterVarsity Christian Fellowship's daily morning prayer groups, their weekend sing-along with prayer, and Saturday morning Bible study. Over two hundred people was a typical turnout for the sing-alongs. This began my Christian community experience, centered on intercessory and contemplative prayer."

"Excuse me for interrupting," said Sam, "but what is contemplative prayer?"

"It is being completely present and open to God in body, mind, and heart. It is prayer without words or images. It is often described as resting in God's presence."

"I get it," responded Sam. "Thanks."

"Today, what spiritually nourishes me is my reading and study of Jungian psychology, mythology, and the theology of many Roman and Orthodox teachers and theologians. I also journal most days and frequently do Active Imagination. I practice contemplative prayer and keep an accurate prayer journal of all intercessory and petition prayers. I have kept this prayer journal since I was seventeen. The prayer journal contains accurate accounts of thousands of petition prayers: when they were prayed, the content of the prayers, when they were answered (yes, no, let it go), and how the prayers were answered. Rereading this journal strengthens my faith in the goodness of God as our Creator and the Lover of our lives.

"I also nurture myself spiritually by initiating and maintaining close relationships.

"My thoughts about death are simple. I believe an afterlife exists. I have studied and taught seminars on the afterlife for thirty years. I have found a deep sense of peace and presence at the death of others and in thinking about my eventual death. I have heard firsthand close to one hundred stories of persons who have had Near Death Experiences. Some shared them at my seminars, while others disclosed their experiences in the privacy of an intimate conversation.

"That is where I am on my journey. Thank you for your interest."

(Applause)

* * *

"Let's take a fifteen-minute break and have refreshments, after which person eight will share his experience," I announced. "Who drew number eight?"

Jim indicated he did.

"Paul, what treat have you made for us?"

"I have fruit kebabs. They contain grapes, melon, blueberries, pineapple, and kiwi. Each is capped with a strawberry."

"Yummy," said George. "Can we have two?"

"Help yourself. There should be plenty for everyone."

JIM'S JOURNEY
The Magnificence of Nature

"Like Hal, I went to the San Diego Zoo this morning. Its lush habitats and thousands of animals in natural settings fed my soul. The zoo is a holy place. It connects me with the awesomeness and majesty of nature. I immerse myself in it as often as I can. My story will make clear why this is so.

"I was born into a French Roman Catholic family in New Orleans. In my family, children's destinies were preordained. One boy was to become a priest, one girl a nun, one boy a doctor, and so on. I was fated to become the priest in my family of two boys and four girls. My older brother was claimed by my father, which left the other five of us to fulfill my mother's dreams of having children devoted to 'God.' My three older sisters were already nuns when my youngest sister sidestepped her 'call' and became a nurse. This was the environment I was raised in, where my path was seemingly set, but my heart yearned for something more, a path that was uniquely mine.

"For high school, I was steered into a seminary attached to and run by a religious order. I grew to love the place because it was located on twelve hundred acres of pine woods and a wonderful river. Another plus was the music. It was glorious. So, I stayed until I realized the place was too small for me. I'd begun reading some of the world's great literature, which convinced me I could no longer stay in that rigid, confining place.

"Leaving the seminary, I carried the beliefs I had been force-fed by my mother since birth. I enrolled at a major southern university, eager to expand my understanding of the world. I devoted myself to philosophy, earning a master's degree. That's when I realized the interminable debates about words and concepts felt hollow. I'd reached the end of that academic pursuit.

"Despite my misgivings, I taught philosophy at two universities to earn a living. While teaching, I developed an interest in Asian philosophy. I traveled a great distance to enroll in a university famous for its courses on Asian philosophy. After a short time there, I embarked on another life-altering journey. I moved to Japan, where I lived with a Zen master in his temple. I followed him when he was made *hojosan*—chief priest—of an ancient Zen Buddhist temple. My two-plus years living in Japan were transformative, clearing my mind of most of the religious—Roman Catholic—beliefs I had been trying to let go of. My health declined, probably due to my diet, so I returned to the States as a changed man.

"My search for a fulfilling career led me to clinical social work. I wanted to do what felt like a good fit for me. I obtained a master's degree and started a private practice that lasted almost forty years. My career was more than just a means of earning a living. It was a continuation of my spiritual journey, a way to apply my evolving beliefs and understanding of human nature to help others. Being a therapist was the fulfilling experience I sought.

"Throughout my professional career, I grappled with a profound internal battle. On one side were the religious beliefs of my upbringing, which I thought had been resolved. On the other side, my evolving understanding of the world. This tug of war led me to delve into the history of religion, particularly the evolution of pagan religion. My studies led me to a conclusion that shook the foundation of my childhood beliefs—Christianity is a continuation of pagan teachings and practices that were prevalent for thousands of years. Since the fourth century, pagan perspectives have transformed into today's Christian church, combining historical myth and the intrinsic need to believe in something.

"Instead of being a Christian, my path brought me to a stunning realization. The true essence of God isn't found in the confines of a church or the pages of a religious text. The true essence of God is found in the incredible magnificence of nature and reality clarified by the laws of science. I embrace reason and the exercise of intelligence, seeing no need for belief in supernatural entities. Therefore, I regard death as not a transition to another life but as a natural part of existence.

"That is why I find the San Diego Zoo a holy place. It is a cathedral that houses the grandeur of nature. It allows me to get out of my head and feel a part of something greater: a higher power, if you will. There are no required beliefs to partake of its beatific essence. Experiencing its transforming presence is available to everyone, offering liberation from the constraints of traditional religious beliefs and a sense of empowerment in finding one's spiritual path.

"I have come full circle in my journey without intending to do so. During my high school days, I lived on twelve hundred acres full of God's beauty and essence, not fully appreciating the grounds are what fed my soul, not the seminary. I moved on to seeking God during my middle years by engaging in philosophical pursuits. Today, I have returned to a conscious appreciation of the magnificence of nature. That's been my path, and I am pleased it led me to where I am."

(Applause)

* * *

"Let's take a five-minute break," I said. "Who's next?"
"I am," said Richard.

RICHARD'S JOURNEY
Embracing Stoicism

"The highlight of my visit to the Midway was listening to an ex-fighter pilot talk about what it was like to be launched off a carrier and the challenge of landing on one. I've seen many films about doing this, but hearing from someone who did it was exceptional. As the pilot said, it was both dangerous and exhilarating. The pilots who do this are remarkable. I am glad I went.

"Regarding my spiritual journey, I grew up in the Episcopal Church. My father was an active member, and I followed his lead. I wanted to please my father and measure up to his expectations. He was a country club kind of lawyer and a prosperous community pillar, but not a nice person. He was an alcoholic. My efforts to please him failed, and I felt I didn't fit in the world.

"I have a brother nine years older than me and twin sisters six years older. My brother was the family prince. He could do no wrong. This left me to be the loser. When I was eight, my sisters were fourteen and interested in sex. They had me get into their pants, which left me feeling used, dirty, and full of shame. It was another indication I didn't fit into my family.

"My grandmother, who was born in Ireland, lived with us. Though she, too, was an alcoholic, her caring helped me survive.

"The Episcopal parish my family belonged to was Anglo-Catholic, meaning it was more Catholic than Protestant. I didn't like their controlling ways or their sales approach to God. Instead, I came to believe a Spirit rules everything and offers help to those

44

in need. We can do anything we put our minds to. We each have our path. Mine, at least until recently, has been ruled by instinct, which always has held me in good stead.

"I attended a high school sponsored by the Episcopal Church. Whenever I went into the chapel, I felt close to God. I also admired one of the faculty members, who was a priest.

"In college, far from home, I had nothing to do with the church. My use of alcohol became a problem. I was a binge drinker.

"I joined the Marines following college graduation. I applied to Tank School but washed out—more proof that I never measured up. I was persuaded to return to the Marine Corps, and this time, I made it through Tank School and went to Vietnam six months later than initially scheduled. The delay was fortunate. I missed the Tet Offensive.

"When I returned from Vietnam, I obtained a law degree, married, and worked for an aerospace company. Drinking remained an active part of my life. When I was in my late forties, my wife divorced me.

"That's when I met the woman who became my second wife. Her positive influence and love enabled me to stop drinking, and life was wonderful."

Richard paused to collect himself.

"My father was dying in Los Angeles. I went to see him and found him in the basement of an assisted living establishment. They kept him there because he was such an angry drunk the other residents wanted nothing to do with him. He was not glad to see me and made me wonder why I made the effort to visit. He was terrified of death and spent the minutes I was with him screaming. I was disgusted and returned home.

"When I retired, I asked myself, 'What is driving my train?' It took me sixteen years to answer that question, but when I did, I knew I'd found the correct answer. Jim will appreciate what I found: Stoicism. Stoicism replaced my religious beliefs with a spiritual one. For those unfamiliar with Stoicism, it dates from about three hundred BCE and is the practice of virtue. The aim is a well-lived life, achieved by practicing daily qualities like courage or temperance. It teaches us to live in accord with nature. To live a good life requires understanding the rules of the natural order. Stoics believe everything is rooted in nature. It teaches the development of self-control as a means of overcoming destructive emotions. Virtue, the highest good, is based on knowledge. The wise live in harmony with the divine reason that governs nature and is indifferent to the vicissitudes of fortune, pleasure, or pain. I constantly ask myself, 'Is this necessary?' Usually, I find it is.

"Because of where I am on my journey, I am accepting of death. I am not afraid because death is part of the grand plan.

"Please speak to me during a break to learn more about Stoicism. I'd be delighted to help you get started."

(Applause)

* * *

"That's it for tonight's presentations," I said. "We'll pick up with Scott, who told me he drew number ten.

"After the clean-up crew finishes, Hal and his new acoustic guitar will lead a sing-along of folk music from the sixties and seventies. His songbook has several new additions. Grab one and join us by the fire."

"I look forward to this every year," said Phil. "What kind of a guitar did you buy?"

"I found a used Martin on sale in a thrift store," Hal responded. "The shop owner didn't know what a fine instrument he had. I bought it at a bargain price, replaced the strings, tuned it, and it sounds marvelous. You can judge for yourself."

"I can't wait to hear it," said Phil.

"The weather forecast calls for rain tomorrow," I said. "Let's make a day out of hearing the remaining journeys. If the rain stops, we'll make other plans. Are there any objections to my proposal?"

"I'm glad everyone will have the chance to share their journeys," said Robert, "but if those of us from the Pacific Northwest let a little rain stop us, we'd never get anything done. I suggest we walk around Old Town tomorrow, rain or shine."

"Is that why you have moss growing on your face?" asked Lawrence.

"That's my beard, stupid," replied Robert. "You're just jealous I can still grow hair!"

"A nice walk in the rain will be good for us," said Peter, "otherwise, we'll just sit all day."

"Okay, I hear you," I said. "We'll make time for those who want to walk in the rain. Does anyone else have a request or suggestion?"

"I do," said Jim. "If there is a break in the rain, I would like to go to the beach. I brought a few of my new kites. It might be a perfect day for kiting."

"That appeals to me," said Mike. "I love the kites you make. It'll be fun to fly one."

"Does anyone want a ride on my Harley?" asked Tim. "I always carry an extra helmet."

"Thanks for the offer," replied Mike, "but I prefer flying kites."

"We'll work an activity or two into the day," I said, "but I want to be sure everyone has a chance to share their story. Let's start singing before the night gets away from us."

SCOTT'S JOURNEY
Navigating the Union of Opposites

"Good morning. As your host, I apologize for the rain. San Diego is not supposed to be like this in May. On the other hand, we're in a cozy room, and the sound of raindrops on the roof and windows adds a soothing backdrop to our presentations. I want to compliment Paul on the mushroom, avocado, and bacon omelets he prepared for breakfast. They were scrumptious. I also heard raves about his homemade granola."

Applause led to a standing ovation. "Bravo!" shouted Peter and Richard. Paul smiled and waved his thanks, his face beaming with pride and gratitude.

"My pleasure," he responded. "I couldn't have done it without Jim."

More applause as Jim stood and took a bow.

"As you take a moment to refill your coffee mugs," I said, "Scott recently achieved an academic milestone. He earned a PsyD, a significant achievement at any age but particularly laudable for an older candidate like Scott. His determination to overcome the challenges he has faced on his healing journey to achieve this accomplishment is a testament to his academic prowess, resilience, and fortitude."

"That's impressive," said Sam. "Well done!"

There was so much chatter I had to ask the group to quiet down. When everyone did, Scott began.

"As the youngest group member, playing pickleball with you older guys showed me I won't have to quit playing anytime soon. It was fun. For old dudes, you played well."

"Thanks for going easy on us," said Peter. "You're clearly the best among us."

"Thank you.

"I've spent much of my life thinking about spirituality and its implications, so I appreciate the opportunity to share my experiences and conclusions with you.

"First, my definition of spirituality. It is the union of opposites. William Blake, a spiritual master I admire, believed there is no progress without opposites. That has been my experience.

"I find spirituality has two sides. One side relates to how each person grows into full personhood through life's polarities (health/ sickness, courage/cowardice, togetherness/aloneness, presence/ absence, attraction/repulsion, etc.). The second side involves our participation in the community Christians call the body of Christ. Most of my presentation will elaborate on these two sides of spirituality.

"You may wonder why I use historic Christian concepts, like the body of Christ. I do because the core Christian symbols still have currency for me. That is, they have an immediacy and electric energy. They are not dead.

"At the center of my spirituality is an I/Thou relationship, which accounts for the love and personal freedom I experience and cherish. It is a loving connection that has shaped my journey and my beliefs.

"The story of my spiritual quest begins with my father and my growing into full personhood. My father was a true Cinderella Man. He fought an existential and mental health crisis every bit as taxing as a boxer—and, I would argue, more so. Dad's opponents weren't in a ring. They energized suddenly out of deep anxiety and other psychological forces most of us can only speculate over. Dad had a psychosis in 1957, which he never fully explained to me. I'll return to his condition and how he battled those ghosts in a moment. This is not an easy story to share."

Scott sat still momentarily, seeming to concentrate on his breathing, sighed, and then resumed.

"My father's influence on my spiritual journey has been profound and dynamic. It has driven me in various directions, fueling or exacerbating my mental health challenges for many years. Dad's influence ranged from moments of inspiration and thoughts of God to genuine horror, from feelings of agape love to moments of pure rage. This was especially true during my younger years. Some of these impacts remain to be healed. Thankfully, we found some peace in each other's presence before he died four years ago.

"A central feature of my unresolved traumatic memories is their tendency to remain stuck in a rigid, almost photographic inflexibility. It is challenging to move forward when you are trapped in the past. As a four-year-old preschooler, my father threw me against my bedroom wall in a fit of rage because he didn't believe me when I told him I didn't break his phonograph records. It was my mother who accidentally broke them."

"Oh, my God," said Steve, his face aghast.

"The impact of that and numerous other traumatic memories stayed with me into adulthood as general anxiety and fear. I still recall how my heart raced in anxiety through my school years when I heard my dad arrive home from work and yell across the house about the garbage or something.

"As a teenager, Dad expressed depressive rage toward me. I called these episodes 'The Curse of Jeff' because he prophesized my failure during these tirades—usually in his underwear on Saturday afternoons. He gritted his teeth and yelled in a scary tone, 'You'll see! When you're older, it will be one failure after another, one thing after another.' My mother finally interceded after I was sobbing. 'Don't do this to him.'"

Heads hung low throughout the group.

"I had no idea," said Sam. "We've got your back now. You're not alone."

"That bastard," snapped George, his nostrils flaring.

"Your support means the world to me. I don't have the words to tell you how much I appreciate each of you being with me on my journey."

Scott wiped away a tear before continuing.

"I was an anxious child diagnosed with high blood pressure by middle school. In the fourth grade, I had to be removed from school for several months due to panic attacks. I felt abandoned, as if God had left me, and I was convinced I would soon die, like my dad's mom, who recently had a heart attack.

"I was instantly cured of this anxiety after only a couple of therapy sessions when I heard my father lamenting in the waiting room how much the sessions were costing. He paid out of pocket. I told him I didn't need to see a counselor and was brought back to school. I now realize neither of my parents talked to me after my grandmother's death. They withdrew emotionally into depression. I was ignored."

"What a crappy childhood," muttered Bruce, shaking his head.

"It wasn't all bad," continued Scott. "I was an All-Conference and All-American defensive tackle football player in college. Unfortunately, my dad never went to a game. He drove me to the stadium several times but didn't come in. He sat in the car reading a book. I took my anger out on the person I felt deserved it most: me. 'I didn't matter,' I told myself."

"Bullshit!" blurted Mike. "Sorry I interrupted, but man, you matter to us. Please continue."

"It was not until my early adulthood that I learned my dad had been involuntarily committed to a mental hospital for two years. During the 1950s, the ECT cures—electroconvulsive therapy—were worse than his disease. To his credit, this Cinderella Man eventually recovered. I respected him for that. He later completed his library science master's degree and became a lifelong librarian, raising five children. I was number two. My father's love of learning was what he did best. He would disappear night after night, reading books or watching reel-to-reel documentaries he brought home from the local college where he worked.

"As I grew older, I saw many of Dad's abusive actions in a new light. After much therapy that lasted into my late fifties, the curse of Jeff became mainly resolved. Today, it's a sad memory of a ridiculous man in his underwear raging at a child who did not deserve it.

"Like many of you, my parents were practicing Roman Catholics. They made sure their children attended Sunday Mass with them. My understanding of God was confused, but I grew to love the devotional practices—prayer, kneeling, readings—each Sunday. There was a poetic structure to the Mass that, as a child, I could not fully appreciate.

"Over the years, I heard some fantastic sermons from old Irish priests. However, it took my adult conversion, which led me to a Protestant seminary in the 1990s, to revive my formerly dented and wrecked spiritual life.

"'Light comes in through the cracks. That was true for me. Whatever was lacking in my relationship with my dad or was un-resolved and needed to be healed was the crack that moments of grace and new father figures shined through and healed me.

"This brings me to spirituality's second side: the body of Christ.

"My dad died just before the worst of the COVID-19 epi-demic took hold. My beloved dog died shortly after that. I was lost while working on an early version of my doctoral dissertation. My soul was adrift. Staring into the abyss, I was blessed to find there was not just darkness staring back at me but a loving com-munity. Memories of seminary mentors who demonstrated how the love of God was creatively embodied and expressed stood out. The miracle of psychological healing has helped me to appreci-ate those men, football coaches, and therapists who acted as true spiritual fathers to me in the absence of my own. These spiritual fathers modeled the courage to 'know thyself' and showed me that agape love has a life-giving dynamic. I integrated this love into my teaching and clinical work. I owe these men my eternal gratitude.

"As I touched on before, football was my religion in college. It was not all hedonism, gluttony, and self-aggrandizement. One of my coaches prayed with the team before games that we would be protected from injury as we sought to play our best. Other coaches didn't pray; those years were godless. Like Steve, I found spirituality to be a slippery slope in the context of elite athletics. In the Gospels, Jesus speaks of the last being first, strength made perfect in weakness, among other teachings. I just knew that if there is a God, he must love football as much as I do!" Laughter filled the room.

"To say my parents were cerebral would be a gross understatement. Football and the team experience opened the door to beautiful emotions in myself and my appreciation for them in others. It would take a decade after football to question the shallow conclusions about God I drew from this period. Free from football's massive distraction, I began to address the more profound spiritual questions that concerned my relationship with God.

"Unfortunately, my father and football weren't my only distractions. Alcohol was also. I became well-versed in the twelve-step programs I attended for about eight years. I now have a healthier relationship with alcohol through God's grace and the personal responsibility instilled by the twelve-step tradition and the group support I received. Life is better sober."

"Amen!" said Phil.

"Totally true," said Richard.

"When it comes to having a spiritual community, I have been influenced by Paul Tillich. He wrote about the courage to be oneself and participate with others. Since my professional life has been of the lone-wolf type, I've been troubled by my lack of working with others. I asked, 'Is this God's will for my life?'

"A good friend who grew up in the fundamentalist Pentecostal tradition responded to my concern. 'As I see it,' he said, 'if you find a good job and it pays the bills or has some purpose—that is God's will.' I took his advice to mean the decisions I make using God-given reasoning and available wisdom are God's will. When I make a wrong choice, God's patience abides. This realization was a blessing.

"Regarding life after death, I find dreams and the occasional insights from moments of deep prayer are my essential teachers. About a decade ago, I dreamed vividly about William James. He believed life's consciousness was separated from an afterlife by a thin veneer. In the dream, James and I walk down a hallway that has windows with wax paper covering them. As we chat, I see people behind the thin layer of wax paper pushing their way as if to get our attention (their hands are going into the thin sheets). I ask James, 'thinnest of veneers, huh?'

"That was the end of the dream, which was more than a little spooky. I was more perplexed about what separates us from another realm when I woke up. I turned to William Blake again. To paraphrase him, I cannot conceive of death as anything other than moving from one room to the next. After my dream, Blake's speculation makes as much sense as anything else.

"One of my most lasting insights came from another big dream. My daughter was near death at that moment. She had been hospitalized after a near overdose and sepsis. I was in shock and emotionally numb after my wife and I visited her and planned her eventual discharge. I had all but given up on her due to the years of her substance abuse and parasuicidal behavior. I had nothing more emotionally to give . . . at least until the following spiritual experience.

"In the dream, I am in tears as I walk alone along the beach at dusk. I look at my wet feet and see torn pieces of a magazine. It is a photograph of a tiger. I lift the pieces out of the receding water and try to assemble them. I weep deeply in that moment of prayer within the dream—I cannot recall ever sobbing like that. I cup the photo's pieces in both hands and look to God, tears pouring down my face. My prayer is simple: 'Please God, put her back together!' Fighting the tears, I look at the tiger pieces in my hands, which burst into flames. I am shaking in the dream as I feel God's healing presence.

"I woke up and wrote down the dream. I have yet to refer to my notes since I still see the imagery in my mind's eye. I share this dream because it has directly and indirectly influenced me.

Directly, it recharged my emotional life. Once again, I felt loving compassion for my daughter. Indirectly, the dream gave me a window into another world with more love, energy, and eternal life than I thought possible. Regardless of the metaphysics involved, this dream and its influence exemplify Eternal Standard Time, a metaphor I use for moments of God's grace. God's grace is Eternal Standard Time, don't you think?"

"I agree," said Hal.

"Over the next several years, my daughter fought hard for her health, mental and physical, and eventually joined a recovery community. She is in her second year, clean and sober, with loving relationships and a career that makes her happy."

"Terrific!" said Peter.

"Experiences like this and the dream highlight one of my favorite observations from Blake, that the voice of God is still active and that voice is love.

"Thank you for listening and for your words of support. I genuinely appreciate it."

"We love you, Scott," said Bruce.

(Applause)

* * *

"Let's take a fifteen-minute break," I said. "Then we'll hear from number eleven."

"That's me," said Paul.

PAUL'S JOURNEY
Created to Create

Paul used the fifteen-minute break to pour himself a cup of coffee, move one of his bouquets to the hearth, and untie his ponytail. When everyone took their seats, Paul began.

"While you were off on your adventures, I stayed here. I'm a local and have done each of these activities, so I didn't need to do one of them again. The time allowed me to do what I love: bake. Making cookies fed my soul, and I'm delighted you liked them. It also allowed me to get a head start on dinner. I'll begin my presentation with my background.

"I have a bachelor's degree in anthropology and a master's in folklore and mythology. As far as my career goes, I've worked as a musician doing studio work for Warner Brothers and nightclub gigs. From 1980 to 2008, I had a business that incorporated flowers, decorations, and a variety of visual aids to homes, hotels, and special events, like the gala I did for the Museum of American History in Washington, DC. From 2009 to the present day, I have been a baker."

"Tell us about the gala," said Bruce, his voice full of curiosity and admiration.

"The Museum was rebuilding its *First Ladies of the United States* exhibition. What had been there was focused on the women's inaugural gowns. For the new exhibit, the curators wanted to shift the focus to the first ladies' changing roles over time. I was commissioned to create the decorations and menu for the opening night festivities. It was an exciting experience, and the curator's new focus was well-received.

"My spiritual journey presentation follows John's suggested topics, so I'll be brief.

"When I was a boy, my parents were evangelicals. We lived in an area that didn't have many churches. The first church I attended was the Free Methodist, though, on occasion, I would attend a Foursquare church for Sunday night services. When I was eight or nine, my father helped start a Southern Baptist church. Our usual schedule was church Sunday morning, Sunday night, and Wednesday night. These early experiences with different denominations launched my understanding of spirituality. They set me on a path of exploration and discovery.

"A positive thing from that period was reading the Bible, which I found fascinating. Reading Scripture was paramount for me, though I had problems with the various churches' interpretations and the regulations they preached. I didn't believe much of what those churches taught by the time I graduated from high school.

"I became involved in the Episcopal Church when I was nineteen. It gave me a different perspective and significantly influenced my journey. The parish I attended introduced me to Jung, Morton Kelsey's books on dreams, and Jack Sanford's writings. Dr. Ollie Backus, an acclaimed university professor, was the volunteer director of religious education. She was my mentor and became a close friend.

"What happened at this parish was revolutionary, even within the Episcopal church. Evangelical churches exposed me to spiritual healing and speaking in tongues. This parish expanded my perspective considerably by showing me an entire mystic reality surrounding us. I experienced exceptional spiritual growth, and it was thrilling.

"Today, I don't attend church that often. Although I love the liturgy of the Episcopal Church, I find the services quite boring.

"There is a Power greater than myself or my ego. Being created in the image and likeness of God, my divineness, or whatever you want to call it, is the primary energy source within my being. I feed this part of myself by meditating, reading, doing activities that benefit others, and seeking beauty. When I am in the presence of beauty, I feel connected to God.

"Spiritual journeys are about creating. We were created to create. Our physical life's main job is maximizing as much creation as possible. That is how I have lived my life.

"Regarding death, I believe that the soul never dies. It is eternal. Our soul is on a journey; we merely enter and leave the physical realm as we evolve."

I interrupted him. "Before you stop, please say more about beauty's role in your journey."

"Happy to.

"In all its forms, beauty plays a central role in my spirituality. I am incredibly blessed to have many talents through which I can express my creativity. When I play the piano, I create beauty through the melodies I play. When I assemble floral arrangements, I create beauty through the flowers' smell, colors, and designs. When baking, I create beauty that both nourishes and people can taste. Each of these acts of creation is a spiritual experience, a connection to the divine through beauty. I derive immense joy and satisfaction from creating beauty, especially when it inspires those around me.

"Jerry Owen quoted on Facebook that 'Beauty is one of the faces of God.' I agree. Owen said, 'Just the act of observing beauty has within it physical, mental, emotional, and spiritual healing powers. We must expect and look for beauty in all things.'

"Beauty is easy to find. I see it in a sunrise or sunset; petting a horse, dog, cat, or even a hamster; when listening to classical music, jazz, or the sound a foghorn from a ship leaving the harbor; when smelling smoke rising from a fireplace chimney, the aroma of coffee brewing, or a bouquet of fresh garden flowers; or when tasting a delicious glass of wine, a favorite dish, or a sample of someone's new creation at Costco. The number of connections to beauty is endless.

"Beauty inspires my creativity. It brings me a sense of wholeness, completeness, and euphoria. It fills me with wonder and awe.
The role of beauty in inspiring my creativity cannot be overstated.
It is a constant and reassuring presence in my life that reminds me
of the divine in all things and keeps me motivated and encouraged
in my creative pursuits.

"Beauty connects me with who I am in my essence, to my
inner Self. It connects me to all there is and all that will be. Beauty
is eternal. It is one of the faces of God. In short, beauty is a constant
and reassuring presence in my life that reminds me of the divine
in all things.

"My journey's path has led me to the numinousness of creation. I thank God for leading me this way."

(Applause)

* * *

"We'll take a ten-minute break before Tim speaks," I said.

TIM'S JOURNEY
The Parable of the Elephant

Tim strolled to the front of the brick fireplace carrying a cup of water, which he placed on the hearth. He looked at some notes he'd made before starting to speak. Tim stood during his presentation.

"I want to acknowledge Scott's pickleball skills. I have been champion of our two-hundred-member league for some time, but Scott is a level or two above my ability. It was humbling playing against you. However, I detected a weakness in your game that I intend to exploit the next time we play."

"In your dreams, Tim," bellowed Scott. "I was simply giving you a chance. Next time, I'll show you no mercy."

Oohs arose across the room, followed by laughter.

"I'm glad you're open to a rematch. Beware, I'm on to you," said Tim, laughing and smiling broadly.

"Thank you, John, for the opportunity to share my experience. I have been impressed by those who have preceded me. They have set a high bar. I will contribute a brief chapter on my journey, reflecting on where I began and am now.

"I grew up in a very traditional home in Northern California. Mom stayed at home while Dad was a hardworking Teamster truck driver. He was a fit, patriarchal, Norwegian physical force of nature. He was 6'2" and 210 pounds. We lived a healthy life with regular meals, a clean home environment, no alcohol or tobacco use, and lots of physical activity. We attended church services regularly: twice on Sunday and at least once mid-week. The family's religious leaning was fundamentalist and conservative. We adhered to a strict moral code. Besides the prohibition of alcohol and tobacco, movies and other 'worldly' endeavors were frowned upon. Like others here, faith healing and talking in tongues were part of the religious lexicon. Sermons on Sunday were fiery and passionate. Pastors and evangelists were almost celebrity-like. This environment profoundly influenced my early beliefs and set the stage for my spiritual journey.

"I was adventurous and active, including riding dirt bikes, camping with my uncles and grandfather, fishing, and roaming the Sierra Nevada mountains with some innocent mischief thrown in. I was a wallflower in school. I participated with mild enthusiasm in school sports: wrestling, football, and pole vaulting. Learning came easy, so I spent minimal time studying.

"High school was uneventful until my junior year. I sat in a Calvary Chapel near our home on a sweltering summer night in the next to the last row. The windows in the sanctuary were wide open to allow in a slight, cool breeze. I was bored. We were attending the third night of a two-week Revival conducted by a reverend from Texas. He was a short, rotund, old-school preacher whose voice boomed as if amplified for a coliseum rock concert. He fell into the 'fire and brimstone' category of evangelical preachers. I still recall a specific line from that night's sermon: 'the world is searching for something, and if we have it and fail to share it with them, then hell is going to be hot for us.' Mom dabbed at the tears that flowed down her face. Dad sat stone faced, arm crossed, with his jaw clenched and a look of resolve. The reverend stormed around the stage like a caged animal, frequently slamming his well-worn Bible on the wooden pulpit as he passed with a loud *thwack*. He moved quickly as if being chased by the law. His voice reached a high-pitched crescendo. His white shirt was soaked in sweat, sleeves rolled up, and his suit jacket had been discarded on the floor thirty minutes ago as he loosened his tie. He delivered the word of God with a vengeance as he waved a sweat-soaked handkerchief, vigorously emphasizing the high notes of every phrase.

His delivery was song-like in tempo and rhyme, and the audience was captivated and teetering somewhere between abject terror and heavenly glory. It was an old-school, tent-revival-like glorious dance between the itinerant evangelist and the devil.

"I sat transfixed by the fearsome potential sentence of eternal damnation I was apparently on track to experience and, at the same time, mesmerized by the theatrical performance of the reverend. I did not comprehend the concept of eternal life shared by my long-dead loved ones, who are in a heaven with pearly gates and streets paved in gold. However, I sure as hell understood the significance of . . . well, hell and eternal damnation. The reverend's voice lowered to an almost whisper as he neared the end of his sermon, and the lights in the auditorium dimmed. He returned to center stage for an appeal, an altar call to the congregants. Everyone knew what was coming. He leaned over the pulpit, held his old Bible out in front of him, and desperately appealed to the unsaved. He was weeping now. Tears flowed down his face in salty streams of released spiritual emotions. He asked the one-hundred-dollar question to a transfixed crowd, now slightly leaning forward in their pews. 'If the Lord were to return right now, as he has promised to do, would you join your friends and family in paradise for eternity? Or would you burn in the lake of fire, forever suffering the torment of Satan and all his demons?'

"I was only sixteen and had yet to learn much about anything life would introduce me to. Still, I was pretty convinced selecting option one, the pearly gates and lions lying down next to lambs, was a better choice than burning in the red-hot lava fires while being tormented by the devil and his apparently really pissed-off cronies. The choice was easy, so I rose to my feet, walked down the long aisle with many other wayward parishioners, and accepted the Lord Jesus Christ into my heart or something like that. Dad walked alongside me for support. I felt like I had dodged a major bullet that night when I finally fell asleep tucked into my twin bed in the safety of my bedroom, a sense of resolution and peace washing over me.

"That was the first step and tipping point in the next chapter of my life, which led me to join the Youth for Christ movement, become a group leader in my high school, and speak to youth groups of all denominations. I left home the summer between my junior and senior year of high school to become an intern in the ministry, which led to teaching Sunday school (nine- to twelve-year-old economically impacted boys), becoming a youth pastor, and eventually an assistant pastor and a youth evangelist, traveling from church to church in my late teens, culminating in being the featured speaker in a youth convention with over two thousand attendees. By twenty-four, I was burned out on the church politics, disillusioned with the inconsistencies between the teachings and the adherence, particularly with the clergy and the leadership. Frustrated, I began to seriously examine my role and the difference between religion and spirituality. I eventually left the ministry and embarked on a few years of rediscovery that included moving to Los Angeles and experiencing much of what Hollywood had to offer with friends in entertainment, entrepreneurs, and the wild and crazy individuals one can encounter in those circles. My journey took me from The Comedy Store in Hollywood to meeting a prince in Dubai, a journey filled with emotional highs and lows.

"It took me a few years to rinse religion out of my system and come to a meaningful and redefined experience with my spirituality. The parable of the elephant and the blind men, reported to have originated in India in approximately 500 BC, best defines my view of God and things spiritual.

"For those unfamiliar with the parable, it is a story of a group of blind men who have never encountered an elephant before and learn and imagine what the animal is like by touching it. Each blind man feels a different part of the elephant's body, but only one part, such as the side or the tusk. They then describe the animal based on their limited experience. Their descriptions varied from one another, so they came to suspect that the others lied, and they came to blows. The story's moral is that humans claim absolute truth based on their limited personal experience as they ignore other people's limited personal experiences, which may be equally valid.

"I have nothing but faith, accepting things I can't prove, and my life experience to frame my views of spirituality and God. Time has taught me that although my spiritual references may be 100 percent accurate, another person may have a completely different understanding, and we both may be correct. Part of my spirituality is simply accepting that as fact. There may be no right or wrong in understanding God; it is just different. I don't rule out any possibility.

"I don't have an answer about an afterlife. I simply don't know. I believe the soul may exist forever, but my spirituality is not guided by a fear of hell or a desire for heaven. Heaven or hell may be right here, right now. I accept the rain that falls or the sun that shines without believing God punishes or rewards me. It just is the way it is. Maybe I die and return to this life more enlightened. Perhaps I die and simply return to earth to become food for the worms. Whatever, I choose to live by a standard that aligns with what appears to be the core tenant of most religious beliefs: to treat others as we wish to be treated. The core of my spirituality is simply to live the healthiest, most fulfilling, most peaceful way I can.

"I believe in Jesus Christ and accept the writings in the Bible are divinely inspired. I don't rule out other divinely inspired writings, teachers, disciples, apostles, and leaders. But if the writings are not divinely inspired, does it matter? The truths therein are the perfect recipe for living a spiritual life and all that entails.

"That said, I am on a journey of learning and understanding God that probably has no defined finish line. Thank you for listening to my experiences and musings."

(Applause)

* * *

"Lunchtime," I said. "Paul, what is on the menu?"

"Grilled chicken, tomato, avocado, and bacon sandwiches on sourdough. I made some of my secret recipe brownies for dessert. Have at it."

"We'll pick up in one hour," I said.

ROBERT'S JOURNEY
God Is Love

"Another fantastic meal from Paul," I said. "I especially loved the brownies. Do you want to tell everyone your secret recipe? We promise not to share it." Laughter rippled through the room.

"Not a chance," said Paul, grinning. "I fund my retirement with that recipe."

"Well, it's a good one," I replied. "Quiet down, everyone . . . Robert is our next presenter. You'll recall he was a Fulbright scholar with a PhD in educational policy. He worked at a major university in the Pacific Northwest. Robert, the floor is yours. Everyone is eager to hear your story."

"I went deep-sea fishing off Point Loma. The captain said we were at a depth of five to six hundred feet. The helpful and friendly crew taught me a lot about fishing. I was surprised by how many fish (mainly bass and rockfish) we caught with so many first-timers on board. It was fun, but I was glad we were out there for only half a day. My stomach could not have handled much more."

"How many did you catch?" asked Sam.

"Two! The crew made it easy. I asked if divers were putting fish on my hook, but the crew said no. I brought back part of what you ate last night. You're welcome." Smiles and chuckles.

"Without question, my mother had the most significant influence on my spiritual development. I'll tell you about that in a moment. Then, I'll share where my thinking has gone since leaving home, how I nourish my soul and apply my beliefs, and conclude with my thoughts about death and eternity. I'll start with memories of my childhood church, where my journey began.

"As a boy, my family belonged to a Disciples of Christ congregation. My mother's parents were long-standing members. I attended Sunday services regularly, evening youth group programs, summer camps, and activities like that. Our family's involvement in the church was a significant part of our lives, shaping my early understanding of spirituality.

"I recall the church was a wonderful worship space. Sweeping steps from the street up to the front door made me feel I was entering a special place, set apart from everyday activities. Inside was a soaring dome above the sanctuary, which contained a balcony above the main floor. Both floors sloped up from the front, like a theater, to ensure no view was blocked, and the curved pews focused everyone's attention on the center. Behind the altar was the choir space, also rising so that the choir could be heard and seen and could lead the congregation in hymns. The pulpit was on the right side of the congregation, raised enough to provide a clear view to everyone. The head pastor was an exceptional preacher, a highlight of every service.

"On the left side of the sanctuary was the total immersion baptistry. I was eight or nine when I was dunked. The entire congregation could see me go under. That is something one remembers." Laughter. "I sputtered, but the pastor's smile was comforting, and I sensed he cared for me. The time I spent at church was good.

"Today, I attend an Episcopal church because I married the daughter of an Episcopal priest, and our daughter is also married to an Episcopal priest. We are currently part of his congregation, which provides me with a supportive and nurturing environment where I can explore and deepen my faith.

"As vital a role as these congregations have played in my life, Mother molded my spirituality. She taught adult Sunday school while I was growing up and was a theologian in her own right. She taught me 'God is love.' When I had trouble believing literally what is in the Bible, Mother suggested substituting the word *love* for every reference to the deity: God, Father, Jesus, Lord, Holy Spirit, etc. This substitution only sometimes works with what Christians call the Old Testament. However, it does work, almost without exception, in the New Testament.

"Here's an example: 'I am the way and the truth and the life. No one comes to the Father except through me,' John 14:6.

"Following Mom's rule, that becomes: 'Love is the way and the truth and the life. No one comes to Love except through Love.' I understand that there are other interpretations of that verse, and many would cringe at the heretical incompleteness of my understanding of God and Christ. Nevertheless, I find comfort in this interpretation.

"Mom's suggestion still works for me and makes me smile whenever I'm called to read at Sunday services. I wish sometimes I could just do the switch, but the rector wants me to hew to the New Revised Standard Version of the Bible—you know, the language Jesus spoke." Laughter.

"Since leaving home, I've sought to identify what I believe. I've read most of the Bible, including all the New Testament more than once, and many parts of the Hebrew Bible. I've done some scholarly reading, but I need a deeper academic understanding of theology to continue my study of Scripture.

"I have been strongly influenced by several writers from the 'search for the historical Jesus' movement, including Marcus Borg and John Dominic Crossan. Their scholarly works have deepened my understanding of Jesus's life and teachings. Other writers, such as the Dalai Lama, C. S. Lewis, Abraham Joshua Heschel, Wendall Berry, and the poet Mary Karr, have also made a strong impression on me, each contributing to my evolving spiritual beliefs.

"It was Wendall Berry who taught me about the essence of God in action. He said it's not a community of believers with a similar outlook that represents God's kingdom on earth, but a community of loving and caring people who make sure everyone in the community knows they are respected and loved, and where differences and oddities within the group are valued and protected. Our group embodies Berry's vision, and I am deeply grateful for your presence and support. It's one of the main reasons I return each year. Paul's cooking is another motivating factor!"

"Absolutely," shouted Andy. Chuckling followed.

"I feed my soul by going to church every week. It reminds me of Jesus's values: love God, love one another, love your enemy, and act out of love. This isn't a mysterious, otherworldly sensation I'm trying to create in myself. It is simply a practical reminder of how I want to live. I have come to this understanding through thought and experience more than a moment of spiritual realization.

"The confession we repeat each week in church reminds me that we can't be perfect and must strive to be less destructive to the world and others. I like the version of the confession that asks forgiveness of 'the evil that enslaves us, the evil we have done, and the evil done on our behalf.'6 It is that last one that cuts me to the quick. I don't slaughter my animals for meat, nor drill for my oil, nor grow all my food, nor make my clothing from the fibers I collect and weave together. In each part of our economic system, some conditions are unconscionably brutal to someone, such as the community—when oil is extracted in the Amazon basin, for instance—or to an animal when it is butchered for food—I do like lamb. Those are the evils done on my behalf, and they seem to be worse—at a minimum, as bad as—any evils I commit directly. It's part of life, I suppose, but living with that realization and trying to make my impact less in that arena is something I think about a lot.

"Participation in ministry also feeds my soul. For most of my adult life, that has meant my career of trying to influence social policy to recognize all individuals with disabilities as full members of the human family. Outside of work, I have volunteered and co-ordinated programs to help homeless and poor people for the last thirty-five years. One of these programs provides essential house-hold goods—like kitchen, bath, and bedroom supplies—and food staples to families moving from homelessness or shelter programs into their first apartment. Another program provides hot meals and sandwiches weekly to three hundred or more needy people.

6. Standing, *Enriching Our Worship*, 19.

"Many loving Christians of different persuasions participate in these ministries, as do others who believe I know not what, some agnostics, and a few atheists. The power of the collective love brought to bear by all these diverse people truly makes a difference. Volunteering, I have met many outstanding members of our local Jewish Temple who are firmly committed to loving one another—including me—and standing for justice and peace as well as any Christian I know. I've gotten to know Muslims and Buddhists who are loving neighbors. One friend's restaurant had its windows smashed early in the anti-Muslim phase of the Trump administration. I saw him at the grocery store and told him how sad it made me to see something like that happen—that I just couldn't understand how people could think that way. He said with sad eyes and a loving smile, 'They are just ignorant. They don't know what they're doing.' From a Muslim, hearing a paraphrase of 'Father, forgive them; for they do not know what they are doing'[7] confirms the universality of love and forgiveness.

"My beliefs change over time as I think about what matters to me. I may be older, but I still think!" Smiles and nodding heads. "I believe in a Power greater than myself, but I have no idea what it is other than love. Anyone who can say they fully know what that greater Power is suffers from hubris. On the other hand, our capacity to unconditionally love another has some spark. That spark underlies all life, particularly in a parent's love for their child.

"Do I believe in God? Yes, but probably not in the way most people think when they hear someone say, 'I believe in God.' The usual terms used to describe belief are not very functional. They hide at least as much as they reveal. So, am I a Christian? I think so, but more in the mold of what a friend described as 'a follower of Rabbi Jesus.'

"So, what do I believe God is? Unknowable in any physical or certain sense. I can't meaningfully separate God from reality. Everything is connected to everything else. Omnipresent might be a good descriptor for God. I agree with our buddy Paul that there is a spiritual dimension to beauty.

7. Luke 23:34.

"I try to be kinder the older I get. There is no satisfaction in being angry at others, including the BMW driver who cut me off in traffic at a merge point." Laughter. "Okay, that used to bother me—now I find it only mildly irritating, not a cause for a contest of wills. As a formerly homeless friend who has overcome the addictions of his past told me, 'Always let the impatient go ahead.'

"My thoughts about death and an afterlife? Who knows? I am not in any hurry." Laughter. "My mother always believed that the 'now we see in a mirror dimly; then we will see face to face'[8] meant that she would fully understand everything when she went to heaven, or whatever it was. That would be nice.

"Friends and family are convinced that the spirits of the dead walk with us . . . in another dimension. Maybe, but it's not a dimension bound by time and space. Christian theology states when Christians die, they go to live in God's eternal kingdom. *Eternal* means something like 'a very long time' or 'without reference to time.' I prefer the second meaning, the absence of time. If eternity is a time-bound and space-bound concept, how could God have been present before creation, and how could God outlast it?

"On the other hand, I have no idea what being in eternity without reference to time would be like, but I suspect that if there is a God, that's where she dwells—using *she* is a little joke; assigning God a gender is more hubris. If death means no longer being in space and time, then eternity is where we end up.

"In short, I have no idea what happens after death. We'll find out when it's our turn.

"You may be surprised that I believe angels exist. Angels are present when someone cares for someone else unselfishly. The angels live in the space—or non-space—between lover and beloved: between the one caring and the one being cared for. This happens in little and sometimes in big, life-risking, life-saving ways. No one is, nor need be, an angel all the time—that's a pretty heavy load—but kindness at every turn and interaction is a good start. Kindness can lead to miracles, another reality I believe exists.

8. 1 Cor 13:12.

"Yes, there are miracles in everyday life. For example, yesterday, I caught two fish. Truly, miracles happen." Laughter.

"Miracles are expressions of God's love, and they amaze me. If the existence of a tree, flower, bird, baby, or lover isn't enough to convince you that miracles exist, indeed, that life itself is a miracle, an expression of God's love, I don't suppose anything will.

"That's where I am on my journey. Thank you for listening."
(Applause)

* * *

"Let's take a ten-minute break," I said. "Who's up next?"
Lawrence sang out, "That would be me."

LAWRENCE'S JOURNEY
Come Here, Get Away

"Lawrence's career was in the United States and Europe's financial worlds," I said. "However, many of us have long suspected Lawrence would have preferred a career on Broadway. I can't thank you enough—or Phil, for that matter—for entertaining us every evening with your singing. It provided a fun change of pace from the presentations." Applause followed. "It's now Lawrence's turn to tell us about his spiritual journey."

Lawrence moved to the front of the room, tipped his Stetson back on his head, and began speaking.

"I wish I could say I enjoyed my time deep-sea fishing, but the swells were strong, and I didn't do well with the motion. Bobbing in the ocean isn't my idea of fun. I didn't barf but was ready to stand on stable ground before anyone else. In the future, I'll stick to ranching."

"Hey, you caught several sea bass," said Andy. "You did better than the rest of us. I think there is a fisherman inside you wanting to come out. I hope you give it another try."

"I don't think so," said Lawrence, laughing. "What I caught was due to beginner's luck, not skill. I prefer spending my day with horses, not fish. That's enough about being at sea; it's time to tell you about my spiritual vicissitudes: my longing for a connection with God that has never been fully realized.

"My parents were Roman Catholic and followed the traditions and doctrines of the church. We attended a beautiful parish in the Bay Area. My three siblings and I were baptized, received our first Communion, and confirmed at this parish.

"However, my only sense of spirituality throughout these years came from admiring the building and its intricate beauty. The recitation of the Mass never resonated with me. I memorized when to kneel, stand, and genuflect in the right places. I went through the motions, but inside there was nothing. During Mass, I spent most of my time looking at the details of the rose window or counting the panes of stained glass throughout the church. Yet, as I know now, I knew then that religion is supposed to be important. I just have trouble connecting to why. This struggle, this silent burden I carry, has been a defining part of my spiritual journey.

"The parish ran a school down the street. My older brother was enrolled so the nuns could 'keep him in line.' Despite the rest of us attending public school, we could not escape the claws of the Catholic school. From first grade through confirmation, we attended catechism classes every Wednesday from 3 to 4 p.m. Of those years, I remember nothing of what I was taught about God. However, I do remember the fifth-grade class. When it came to catechism classes, everyone looked forward to the course taught by Missus Christiansen. Compared to the droning nuns, Missus Christiansen was sweet, fun, and passed out candy at the end of each class. At the end of the school year, Missus Christiansen invited everyone to her house for a pool party. I don't remember anything she taught us, but I remember her 1964 Lincoln Continental with the suicide doors. That car was cool." Chuckles erupt.

"The rector of the church and school was a lovely man, but he was old and uninspiring. His assistant was soft spoken and gentle but spoke in a monotone voice when he gave a sermon or, heaven forbid, substituted for one of the nuns in catechism class. He was awkward, stuttered, and was equally uninspiring. All the kids referred to him as Father Inane, and I've always felt bad about that. The priests' lack of inspiration contributed to the void in my early religious life.

"I recall only one sermon ever making an impression on me. It was Mother's Day, and the rector spoke. He said something that has stuck with me. 'Give your mother flowers when she can enjoy and appreciate them,' he said, 'rather than place them on her grave when she will not.' I tried to do that whenever I could.

"The parish had no choir, Sunday school, or youth social activities. You just went to Mass, did what was expected, and went home. It was very dull. I was done when I entered high school, turned off by the parish's lack of outreach to young people.

"I was involved in musical theater during high school. Many of my friends went to a Presbyterian church and were members of their choir, which consisted of about sixty voices. This church had a youth minister and activities, but the choir caught my attention. The Presbyterian program better suited my interests.

"Each summer, their choir would go on a two-week tour. In my junior year, the tour was through Southern California, Arizona, and New Mexico. I joined the choir for the trip and the adventure. We performed a contemporary show called *Celebrate Life*. It told the story of Jesus, from immaculate conception to crucifixion. This musical was not just a performance but a revelation, teaching me more about the Christian faith, Jesus, and God than all the masses and catechism classes I'd attended. The experience of participating in the musical and understanding the story of Jesus in a new light was a turning point in my spiritual journey.

"One place the youth choir performed was on the South Rim of the Grand Canyon. We stood on risers in front of vast windows overlooking the canyon. I could feel the grandeur behind me even at night, facing away from the windows. Leslie, with an angelic soprano voice, was cast as Mary. She stepped off the risers into the spotlight during the show that night. Then softly, she began to sing, her silhouette in bright white light. I was overwhelmed. The sheer power of the moment was so intense that my knees buckled, and I fell backward from the top riser. Thankfully, the guys on both sides caught me and held me firmly.

"I have always considered this a spiritual experience. It was, and still is, the most potent spiritual feeling I have ever had. The combination of the breathtaking natural scenery, the powerful performance, and the overwhelming emotions I felt all contributed to a profound connection to God and awe. I yearn for this connection in an ongoing way, which hasn't happened yet. My journey has been a series of ups and downs, like bobbing at sea.

"After graduating from high school, I drifted away from church, religion, and any thoughts of a spiritual life. The lack of engaging youth activities, the dull worship, and the absence of a strong connection with the parish contributed to my disengagement. The activities that did attract me led me elsewhere.

"In my late twenties, I struggled to find direction and a way out of the deep financial hole I'd dug for myself. I don't recall how it came about, but I read the book *Try God* by Laura Hobe. It made a powerful impression on me, and I firmly embraced God and Jesus, at least for a while. It didn't spark a need to attend church, and I don't recall reading other related books. *Try God* awakened me to the idea that seeking a relationship with God would strengthen me and make me a better, happier person. But that's where it stopped. I relocated and became caught up with the distractions I found in my new home and place of work. Seeking a relationship with God got moved to the sidelines.

"Fast forward another ten-plus years to when I met my wife. She was involved with a Presbyterian church and had built a friendship with the pastor and his wife. Occasionally, I attended services with her and her children from a previous marriage. I felt comfortable during the services but never felt the need to dig deeper into developing my faith. We were married by the pastor and stayed connected to the church.

"A year later, we moved to California. We still had a long way to go to become a family. The children were eight, twelve, and fourteen. I thought it would be good for us to find a church home where, as a family, we could build a connection with the community around positive Christian values. My wife was on board with the idea even though neither of us missed the spiritual aspects of church life.

"We checked out the local Presbyterian church, but it wasn't what we wanted. A friend suggested we try the United Methodist church. A new pastor had recently arrived, and we liked him.

We began attending services regularly, most of the time with the children. Things seemed to be going well until a schism developed in the church over the pastor's approach to church doctrine. I don't recall the details. The rift resulted in half the congregation leaving with the pastor to form a new congregation. We followed them, and all was fine until one Sunday, the pastor's sermon denounced gays." Many groans crossed the room. "The pastor's words offended my wife, which ended our participation with that congregation.

"We shopped around for a new church but never found a good fit. After sampling four or five alternatives, our efforts faded. From time to time, I would feel the urge to go to church, but not being connected to one, I defaulted to the familiar and went to Mass. Our neighbors were devout Catholics, and I attended their parish for a while. But again, I didn't feel any spiritual growth from the experience and eventually stopped going.

"After we moved to Southern California, I again wanted to find a church home. It would be an excellent way to meet new people and become part of a community. We went to two different Presbyterian churches, one small and the other large. The small one was nice but a bit pushy in their recruiting style. I preferred the larger one. My wife wasn't as enthusiastic. She thought it was a bit of a 'happy clappy' church and preferred a more traditional service. Once again, we drifted away from searching.

"One day, I was reading the newspaper and saw an article about the new rector at an Episcopal church. 'Hey, look,' I said to my wife, 'the new priest is from London.' That's where my wife was born. 'Let's check him out.'

"My wife was comfortable with the familiar Anglican service. She enjoyed the fantastic choir and singing hymns she grew up with. I found the order of service much like the Catholic Mass. I began to think of the experience as 'Catholic Lite.' I described the Episcopal Church to my family as the 'Catholic Church without the guilt.' Today, my wife rarely attends services. I go a couple of times a month, sometimes serving as an usher or reader, and I participate in two social service ministries.

"So far, my presentation has been more of a chronology of my church life than a description of my spiritual journey. That's because I've been unable to find what I've sought.

"I described my spiritual journey to the Episcopal rector this way. It is like standing outside of a warm and comfortable family-style Italian restaurant. I look through the window at happy diners enjoying a rich and flavorful meal. I want to join them, taste and savor the satisfying meal they are enjoying, but something holds me back. I'm afraid to go inside, fearful of what will be required of me, scared to entirely give in to what the meal promises.

"I finally step inside the door and ask to see a menu. I look at the prices, survey the tables, and look for an open seat that suits me. The restaurant is nearly full. Still, there are tables available. The hostess asked if I would like to join them. I hesitate and then reply, 'Perhaps another time.' I leave. Back outside, I could still smell the tantalizing aromas of the hearty food and hear the contented voices of happy diners. I'm missing a great meal.

"I've known a few people who were like the diners in the restaurant. They appear to have a deep and fulfilling relationship with God that blesses them with peace and contentment. I want that. At the same time, their depth of spiritual fulfillment makes me uncomfortable. I feel less of a person for not measuring up to their spiritual status. They are more worthy than I—holier, if you will. I know intellectually that this isn't true. After all, everyone's spiritual journey is different.

"My pursuit of a relationship with God has been one of 'Come here, come here—go away, go away.' My wanderings toward and away from church life reflect my half-in-half-out effort. I want in, but not all the way. I want to have a rich relationship with God, but I'm not willing to do the work to read, hear, and study God's word. I want an unquestionable faith in Jesus and the story of his birth, death, and resurrection. Unfortunately, I don't have that full measure of conviction. Still, I accept Jesus's story based on the faith I have.

"Between 2017 and 2022, I made a broader effort to learn, pray, and connect with God. My dear friend Jim was battling cancer and encouraged me to read a daily devotion with him. Sometimes, I would pray after reading, and Jim sent me texts commenting on the day's reading. I found the routine an excellent way to start the day and to have fellowship with my friend, who was hundreds of miles away. The practice expanded to include reading something spiritual but not necessarily religious. For example, I read all of Og Mandino's books and all of Mitch Albom's books. When my mother had her accident and emergency brain surgery in 2018, my faith gave me strength through her ordeal and beyond her death in 2019. The practice of reading a daily devotional waned over time, especially after Jim died in 2020.

"I would restart the practice occasionally, then stop when the routine was broken by going on one trip or another. Like building an exercise routine, once you skip a day or two, it's easy for the whole thing to disappear. The same pattern followed with attending church services.

"When my brother became ill and died in 2021, I'd fallen out of the practice of daily spiritual reading. Later, I tried to restart the practice but found it harder to get into.

"This has been frustrating to me. I've always felt like I was missing out and needed to try harder. I needed to devote more time and effort to building my spiritual life. And that may be the case. And perhaps one day I will.

"The ebb and flow of my spiritual journey continues. I am becoming more content with my limited approach to seeking a relationship with God. I'm taking pressure off, not pushing myself to reach a higher sense of fulfillment and faith. For now, I will be satisfied with loving God as fully as I can, showing up at church now and then, acting on opportunities to serve others, reading for spiritual enlightenment, and growing in faith as I continue my journey.

"Turning to death and dying, I'm not afraid of death, but like Robert, I'm in no hurry for it to happen, either." Chuckles. "I am scared about how I might die. I fear dying in bodily pain, suffering, and feeling alone. If that should be my fate, I pray that God will be by my side and I will feel his presence. I am grateful not to have experienced these kinds of deaths among my friends and loved ones.

"In a few cases, my loved ones' deaths were abrupt. My father ate a big bowl of ice cream, went to bed, and didn't wake up. A beloved aunt had a massive heart attack sitting in her living room chair and was gone. Don't we all wish that we would go that way?"

"You betcha," said someone I couldn't see.

"I am up in the air—no pun intended—about what happens after we die. I want to believe, and choose to believe, in the promised afterlife of a heaven full of joy and beauty beyond my comprehension. I choose to believe I will be reunited with loved ones who have died. Beyond the joy of a reunion, I will discover my faith in God has been rewarded in the abundance of the promised land.

"I struggle with the ideas of hell and purgatory I was taught as a child. I appreciate that these are not a focus in Protestant denominations. I also have a problem with the idea that God would deny entry into heaven to anyone who believes, praises, and glorifies him but does not accept Jesus as Lord and Savior. I find it hard to believe that God, who loves all his children, would turn away Jews, Muslims, Hindus, Buddhists, or anyone who believes in him but not in Jesus. How can that be?

"I am also open to the idea that when you die, that's it. That's the end of it. There is nothing that comes after. We are all part of the life cycle, a cog in the ever-spinning wheel of nature.

"As with most of my spiritual journey, I've never been inclined to do the heavy lifting of studying the Bible, engaging in conversation, or researching Christian doctrine to satisfy my questions or reservations.

"And maybe that is why I'm stuck in an endless cycle of 'come here, come here—get away, get away.'"

(Applause)

* * *

After a pause, I asked Paul what snack he had prepared for us.

"I have warm churros with sugar lightly sprinkled over them. There's vanilla ice cream to go with the churros. Help yourself."

79

"You have my mouth watering," I said. "I'm told the rain has stopped. Let's take a break from presentations and pick up after dinner."

"I'll bring out the six kites I made and brought with me," said Jim. "I think we should fly them at the beach."

"My car will hold five people plus me," said Mike. "I'll drive a group to the beach."

"My car will hold the same," said Peter. "I'll meet you out front in fifteen minutes."

Sam volunteered to lead a walk around Old Town, while Hal offered to do the same at Balboa Park.

"Dinner will be at 5:30," said Paul. "Don't be late."

"Before everyone leaves," I asked, "who drew number fifteen?"

Bruce raised his hand and headed for the churros.

BRUCE'S JOURNEY
Like a Roller Coaster

The men animatedly shared their experiences from the outings over a delightful dinner of chicken shawarma, rice, tomato and cucumber salad, and flatbread. The lively crosstalk led to the decision that a representative from each group would give a brief report, which added to the evening's enjoyment.

Richard spoke for the kite flyers.

"First, Andy is fine. He tripped over a rock while looking up at the kite he was flying. He scraped his knee, and his back was sore from landing on other rocks. He's more embarrassed than physically hurt."

"I'm okay," said Andy. "I didn't hit my head or break any bones. I'd prefer we not discuss it anymore since I'm fine. Even the kite survived my tumble."

"Speaking of the kites," said Richard, "Jim's were fun to fly, especially in the stiff breeze. They were the talk of the beach. People appeared out of nowhere to see them. The surfers even stopped to watch. Everyone had a good time, and Jim sold two kites!"

Hal reported on those who went to Balboa Park.

"We chose to spend our time in the Japanese Friendship Garden. The path through the winding garden was paved, so no one's shoes got muddy. My favorite sights included the dry rock garden, with its raked sand that invited me to meditate; the koi ponds, which added life and color to the garden; and the bonsai exhibit. I'm a sucker for bonsai trees, especially the ancient ones. They are living works of art. Seeing them is a spiritual experience. I'd like to return for the cherry blossom festival. I imagine the garden is even more impressive when it is in bloom."

Sam spoke for those who walked Old Town.

"The visit to Old Town was a trip back in time, particularly to the nineteenth century, with the various homes and businesses on display. Everyone's favorite was the Whaley House. Initially a home for the Whaley family, it became San Diego's first theater and later a courthouse. What makes the Whaley House fun is its reputation for being haunted. The structure was built on a former gallows site, and tourists there after dark regularly testify to encountering ghosts. We didn't, but restorers of the property noticed unusual and mysterious sights, sounds, aromas, and encounters. Besides those who died on the gallows, several Whaley family members died in the house, one by suicide. The house is said to turn cold when she is present. Visitors have smelled the French perfume worn by another Whaley woman. We also visited Heritage Park to see six restored Victorian homes and San Diego's first synagogue, Temple Beth Israel. The attractive holy place tugged at my heart as I thought about the men and women who have worshipped there. They were keepers of the faith in a foreign land."

"Thank you, gentlemen, I said. "It sounds like everyone had a good break. Now, it's time for Bruce to share his journey."

Bruce put down the cigar he was chewing, spit into a bottle, and walked to the front of the room.

"I went to the Japanese Garden. The only thing I'd add to Hal's report is the variety of birds I saw. I noticed the typical crows, sparrows, and finches, but I heard a mockingbird and spotted a circling hawk. That was more than I anticipated and added to my enjoyment. I'm glad I went. I'm sorry about your spill, Andy. I'm happy you're okay.

"My spiritual journey has been like a roller coaster—slow, methodical, and smooth at times—and out of control during others. I will try to recreate it as it happened—chronologically—beginning with my birth and early years in Los Angeles's San Gabriel Valley. Little did I know the twists and turns that awaited me.

"I was baptized in an Episcopal church for reasons known only to my parents. My brother and I attended Sunday school at the Presbyterian church, which was comfortable because we knew most of the kids. We went there until we were old enough to join the Boy Scout troop the local Lutheran church sponsored. We continued in the Boy Scout and Explorer programs until about fifteen or sixteen. During my teen years, my only religious exposure was an infrequent scouting event with the Lutherans at their church. My parents did not attend church. However, they encouraged my brother and me to find comfort in our religious lives. In other words, they did not force religion upon us.

"As a senior in high school, I dated Debbie (not her real name). Debbie was born and bred Roman Catholic. She attended Catholic school and church regularly through the eighth grade and practiced her faith at home with her family. Our relationship and her faith significantly impacted my spiritual journey, but not immediately.

"After high school, Debbie and I went our separate ways. She went on to junior college, dated different guys, and worked for the hometown newspaper. She also continued her religious education and practice.

"I went to a different junior college, joined a fraternity, and made new male friends. I worked various jobs and dated multiple women before transferring to a major university. I graduated with a BS in journalism. Throughout my college years, I didn't practice any religion or attend services of any denomination.

"Debbie and I got back together during my senior year of college. After graduation, I went to the US Navy Officer Candidate School. As the Vietnam War accelerated, I was commissioned ensign in the US Navy Reserve. I reported to a cruiser homeported in Norfolk, Virginia, where I was the public affairs officer. I enjoyed my assignment aboard the USS Northampton, the president's flag ship.

"Debbie visited me in Norfolk. We bought a car together and talked about marriage. I proposed, and she accepted. I returned to the San Gabriel Valley for Christmas, and we made plans to wed the following August twenty-sixth. I agreed to raise our children in the Catholic Church. I returned to Norfolk, and Debbie planned the wedding.

"All was well until August twenty-first, when my ship received orders from the Joint Chiefs of Staff, to whom it reported. We were to proceed to New England and await further orders. Suddenly, my wedding was in jeopardy. In Maine, we picked up President Johnson, many senators, representatives, and governors, along with their wives, for an overnight trip to Canada. Fortunately, I could board a helicopter off the ship and travel to Southern California. I met with the parish priest to receive an 'education' about marriage that non-Catholics must have before the ceremony.

"Debbie and I married as scheduled and had three children during the next five years. Over the next twenty-nine years, there were eighteen moves to/from England, Vietnam, Japan, and Hawaii. We moved to/from San Diego four times as I finished my assignments. I worked for the next twenty-one years for the Naval Investigative Service, followed by a short career with the Drug Enforcement Administration.

"Most of my spiritual roller coaster ride took place during my marriage. Our children went to Catholic school through eighth grade, and I did not oppose this. They attended frequent, if not weekly, Catholic services with Debbie with no opposition from me. I attended periodic and special occasion Masses with the family—perhaps six or eight times yearly. During a two-year assignment in Okinawa, Japan, Debbie attended Masses more than twice a week, along with religious education classes, special church programs, or other Catholic activities probably three more days per week, enough so that it caused friction in our marriage.

"I was ready to change my lifestyle when we returned to San Diego. The change came from two events that originated from the same source: an exceptional Catholic neighbor. First, he invited me to help plan and execute a monthly men-only prayer breakfast. I immediately became involved and remained a key member for over twenty years. This event prompted me to meet and become friends with other men in the parish, which provided meaning to a new word in my vocabulary—*service*—to my fellow man.

"The second event the neighbor proposed was a couples' weekend at a Christian family camp. Several new friends and some old parish friends were there. Two couples who participated led the effort to locate, purchase, build, and staff the only Catholic family camp in the San Diego area, Whispering Winds. I became involved in the process, including financial support, and continue to do so.

"Debbie's and my participation in the family camp and my new attitude toward the Catholic Church prompted our neighbor and his wife to sponsor us for a Catholic Cursillo weekend. Cursillo was a growing movement that got people involved in practicing faith in everyday activities. Debbie readily agreed to participate; I reluctantly agreed. Cursillo was structured so men attended one weekend, and their wives attended two weeks later. I was made a table captain at my weekend as one of the few non-Catholic participants. The service and instruction provided by the Cursillo team overwhelmed me. I made a public commitment to join the Catholic Church. Much of the weekend was public knowledge, but several significant events were designed to surprise. The following two weeks were pressure filled as I held secrets close to my heart. Debbie proclaimed her pleasure in attending the event and making many new friends.

"Cursillo became an essential ingredient on our calendar for many years. Debbie and I became members of the teams created to put on the Cursillo weekends—commitments that required months of meetings, devotion or lecture preparation, and financial support. Additionally, there were weekly get-togethers to discuss our religious study and evangelical actions. Cursillo music became important to me. I loved many songs: "How Great Thou Art," "De Colores," "Be Not Afraid," "Here I Am Lord," "One Bread, One Body." They still do something for me when I occasionally get a chance to sing them at a funeral or church function.

"Beyond the vast changes Cursillo brought into my home, I had committed to join the Catholic Church. That entailed registering with the first rite of Christian initiation of adults program. Eight to ten people attended Mass faithfully for the next eight months, usually while serving as ushers. The next few years were the most spirited, enjoyable years of my adult life.

"Ironically, the more involved I got with the Catholic Church and Cursillo, I thought to please Debbie, the more distanced our marriage became. In the early 1990s, my job took Debbie and me to Hawaii for two years without our adult children. Although we regularly attended Masses, we did not have the parish community we'd had for so many years or the involved Cursillo people to keep us on the right track. We were stranded in a strange land with few friends and no loved ones. We returned to San Diego, and I retired from NCIS one year later. Debbie and I stayed together for eight more years before divorcing in 2002. Our marriage ended after nearly thirty-seven years."

"That's really sad," said Sam.

"It is," said Mike, shaking his head.

"I continued doing the same thing that gave me the little spiritual strength I needed—regular church attendance. But our divorce forced me to move to a different home, parish, and people. I began losing my friends, and this has continued. Funeral after funeral after funeral—mainly Catholic friend after Catholic friend after Catholic friend. In time, I lost my Cursillo identity and association.

"I have since married a wonderful woman who is well-grounded in all good things except spirituality, at least the physical practice of it. She doesn't pray or desire to attend services. We enjoy doing many things together, but religious life is not among them. We attended three Catholic churches in the first ten or twelve years of our relationship. None provided the companionship and spirituality I found in my former parish. None offered whatever my second wife was looking for, and we gradually lost interest and quit attending, partly because of the COVID issue. I have lost much of the spirituality I gained forty years ago. I sometimes find it when I lose a good friend or face a significant problem or issue.

"Social interaction is hugely important in the framework of spiritual satisfaction. Friends, contacts, group activities, different people, and different things are all necessary to balance personal life issues. I have had numerous groups of people doing different things in different places where I have different roles in my inter-actions, providing different satisfactions. Some groups I partici-pated in—like Cursillo and the men's prayer breakfast—were part of the religious community and instrumental in my spirituality. Religion in my other groups, like our fantasy baseball league or neighborhood groups, while comprised of like-minded people or Catholics, played only a passive role in our activities. Other groups, like work-related organizations, Little League baseball, or my new neighborhood walking group, have been great for social interac-tion and developing friendships but aren't suitable for religious or spiritual growth.

"I don't spend time thinking about death and the afterlife. I don't understand them, so I'd rather not say anything.

"To summarize, roller coaster is a pretty accurate word to de-scribe my spiritual journey. The most instrumental people in my early life, my parents, did nothing to promote religion for me. In my mid-life, I found a community—rather, the community found me—that brought spirituality into my everyday life. Now, in later life, I am on the edge without a religious base, but still with family and friends to keep me energized and happy. That has been my spiritual journey."

(Applause)

* * *

"Let's take a fifteen-minute break," I said. "There are two pre-sentations remaining. Sam is up next."

SAM'S JOURNEY
Repairing the World (Tikkun Olam)

S am's large stature caught everyone's eye. He walked with his head held high, his thick, grey hair wild and unbrushed, like Einstein's. Sam's beard was full but not long like an Orthodox Jew's. His long arms reminded observers of professional basketball players. Without saying a word, Sam commanded attention. He stoked the fire and then began speaking.

"Contemplating my spiritual journey enabled me to explore how I experience G-d and my Jewish faith. I don't view my life experiences as profound or extraordinary. Whether it's family, health, financial, or other challenges, they were just parts of my life.

"I was born in Los Angeles. Our house was in a post-war community with many young families. Dad was a carpenter, a tradesman like the rest of his family, and Mom, unlike most of the mothers in the community, wasn't a housewife. She taught dance. I didn't realize a working mom was unusual. I thought moms worked just like dads. Mom opened her dancing studio in our garage. Dad added ballet bars and mirrors to the walls. Every afternoon, Mom would teach while Dad did his carpentry.

"Construction work was not constant, and Dad was often out of work. It wasn't until I was a little older that I realized Mom's dance studio was something she loved and necessary for our financial well-being. After a few years, Dad got a job with the Los Angeles school district doing maintenance and construction. This was great: full-time employment with benefits—a steady paycheck and a secure job. The pressure was off Mom, although she continued to teach.

"This led to one of the first religious conflicts I experienced. My family was very musical. My sister and I took music lessons and danced. My sister is five years older and better than me. I didn't understand I might be as good in five years—just that she was better now. Anyway, I sang in the elementary school choirs and played bass in the orchestra. As we prepared for the Christmas show—this was the early 1960s, so it was not yet the winter show—I was very involved. Two weeks before the show, Dad announced he'd been fired because he was Jewish. This was devastating. Even at a young age, I saw the conflict of singing in a Christmas show when Dad had been fired because he was Jewish.

"With this anger, I refused to sing or play the bass at the next rehearsal. I sat by myself in the center of the empty auditorium. The music teacher came over to ask what was wrong. I told her Dad was fired because he was Jewish, and I wouldn't participate in the show. She immediately went to the principal and asked her to talk to me. I told her what happened, and she made a deal with me. She would find out what happened if I would participate.

"Unbeknownst to me, the principal called Mom a few days later and asked her to come in. The principal told Mom she had investigated what happened. Dad, far from being fired because he was Jewish or the result of any anti-Semitic actions, had been fired because he was spending too much time watching the school kids—especially the little girls. This put the principal in a difficult position. It became Mom's job to tell me about the firing. It wasn't till many years later I found out the real reason.

"Nonetheless, this episode helped me feel more assertive about my Jewishness—even if Dad lied. I understood I could stand up for my religious beliefs—especially as a minority religion. It made going to the temple on Friday nights, religious school on Sundays, and preparing for my bar mitzvah all the more important. It made the holidays and the family gatherings at Passover and Hanukkah much more meaningful. I wasn't more religious, just more steadfast about being a Jew.

"In the fifth grade, a schoolmate got mad at me and called me a dirty Jew. I was so angry I slugged him and ran home. All eventually resolved itself, but as with being told erroneously that my father had been fired because he was Jewish, having a schoolmate call me a dirty Jew shocked me. Instances like this made me a more resolute Jew. More spiritual or observant—I don't know.

"My father was the sixth of seven children. By all accounts, he was good-looking and charming. He was a big man—especially to a little boy. He worked on major construction projects—like a fifteen-story hospital about a mile from our house. I remember standing in the middle of my schoolyard at an appointed time to wave to him supposedly standing on the top of the hospital under construction. I swore I could see him return my wave. He also built many house add-ons, including a significant addition to our house. To this day, I have a bunch of his tools I relish holding and using, just as he did so long ago.

"My relationship with Dad was always good. As the youngest of two kids, I was more manageable than my sister. Dad's relationship with her was complicated, and I was oblivious. I just did my stuff and saw little of the family difficulties—of which there were many. When I was nine and my sister was fourteen, she attempted suicide. I only knew she was upset and troubled. I had no idea she was acting out the rocky and sometimes physical—though not sexual, as far as I know—aggressiveness Dad showed her. About two years later, Mom decided to divorce Dad for a variety of good reasons that were all well beyond my understanding as an eleven-year-old.

"My only vivid memory of him from that period was sitting in the car he packed to leave the house for the last time. He said talking to me about the birds and the bees was vital because he was leaving. Not that I understood much of what he was referring to—again, I'm eleven—but I guess he felt it his fatherly duty before he left. I've always thought that being told about sex at the same time your parents are separating was not the healthiest forum for this conversation. Oh well." Subdued chuckles oozed from the group.

"After Dad left, we didn't see much of him. I remember he took my sister and me to the movie *Father Goose* with Cary Grant and Leslie Caron. Indulging my early analytical mind, I calculated I'd spent, on average, about twelve minutes a day with him since he left. Sometimes, analysis is not the best thing to do.

"By the beginning of the following year, Dad moved to Hawaii, the place of his greatest fun and independence when he was a young man—even though it was wartime. He was in Hawaii on December 7, 1941, and was reported lost for two weeks—another story.

"It wasn't for another four or five years that he returned. Dad didn't call us when he got back. My now stepfather, with whom Dad was a friend—that too is another story—asked him to call. Dad didn't. It wasn't until I called him that we finally spoke. Over the next few months, we visited until he died suddenly of a heart attack.

"Growing up, our family was friends with many other families at our temple. I would stay with one family's two boys—older than me—while our parents danced. Over time, however, the husband and wife of the two boys had problems and divorced. The husband became close friends with Dad and Mom. The problem was Dad was not as hardworking and responsible as their friend was. As kind and caring as Dad was not, the other fellow was. As generous as the other man was, Dad was happy to accept that generosity. As my parents moved closer to divorce, this other man remained friends with Dad but got even closer to Mom. A few years after my parents divorced, Mom married this other man, who was a great parent to me. He showed me how to be a good stepparent.

"It surprised everyone to learn our families became acquainted through our temple. His last name was Italian; he was a large man who could be loud and intimidating. As a boy, he'd been raised as a Roman Catholic but converted to Judaism while in Europe during World War II. As the story goes, his first wife was Jewish, and they married a few weeks before he left for Europe as an army private. This was at the start of World War II. Once in Europe, he realized being married via a civil ceremony to a non-Catholic who could very well be pregnant might be a problem. He asked a combat priest how the Catholic Church would view a child born to his distant wife. The priest said that because the child would be born to what the church regarded as an unmarried woman, the child would be considered a bastard. This made my future stepfather very angry. He was risking his life to fight against the Nazis, who, along with Mussolini, were attacking the Catholic Church, yet the Catholic Church would view his child as a bastard.

"He went to a rabbi and asked how Jews would view the status of a child born to a mixed marriage without a rabbi. The rabbi responded that for Jews, there was no problem. Jews believe that a child born to a Jewish mother is Jewish. My future stepfather, angry at the Catholic Church, appreciated the Jewish perspective and initiated his conversion to Judaism while fighting in Europe. He completed his conversion after the war and remained an observant Jew till his death. I was inspired by his choosing to be Jewish. He raised his two sons Jewish, supported me through my bar mitzvah, and attended the temple for the rest of his life. A Jew with an Italian last name was odd, but he was a welcome member of our temple.

"Our religious life as I grew up was typical for reformed Jews in Southern California. You went to Friday services regularly but not Saturday morning. You attend Sunday school and start Hebrew school at nine in preparation for your bar mitzvah at thirteen. My sister chose not to be bat mitzvah. We celebrated the Jewish holidays as a family. We went to services for Rosh Hashanah and Yom Kippur. Passover provided a fun seder, held at my maternal grandparents' apartment, my aunt's house, or our home, each presenting a festive setting. Hanukkah was always an eight-day occasion to light candles, get presents, and eat tasty traditional Jewish foods. I loved the holiday celebrations. They brought me closer to my family and religious roots.

"Again, Judaism focused on the traditions and history of the Jews and how, through our daily actions, celebrations, or attendance at religious ceremonies, we defined ourselves as Jews. Maybe if we were Conservative or Orthodox, there would be a greater leaning on belief, spirituality, responsibility, obligation, or even guilt. But as Reformed Jews, we looked for the balance of being a Jew and integrating into the greater community, which shocked us when we experienced anti-Semitism.

"East Coast Jews were more integrated into the immediate community, making observance easier. This wasn't the West Coast Jew's experience. In California, temples were not within walking distance, kosher food was impossible to find, and communities were predominantly Catholic or Protestant. West Coast Jews had to redefine themselves. We believed at the heart of Judaism was our obligation to better the world—*tikkun olam*, Hebrew for 'repairing the world.' That is what belief and spirituality meant for me—acts to better the world. Whether doing a simple good or generous deed or helping to house homeless families at our temple, these were more spiritual to me than most anything experienced in the temple or at the seder table.

"Until recently, spirituality, as I conceived of it, raised people to another level of thought and belief, consciousness, or existence. My impression of other people's spirituality was a religious revival meeting or in a Southern Baptist church with eyes fluttering and hands raised to touch the hand of G-d. That's never been my world.

"My spirituality is focused on personal introspection and community involvement. Going to the temple provides me with a physical environment where I can look within myself in the same sanctum used by generations and share with others our place, role, and responsibilities to the world. While being in the temple is not a prerequisite, the temple environment provides me with a context that helps.

"My view of spirituality changed as I experienced Jewish occasions with my two grandchildren. To see them recite the prayers, eat challah, or light the Shabbat candles brings more to me than the satisfaction of the continuance of a heritage. It's something significant—something akin to spirituality.

"Two life events have had the most significant impact on my life: being diagnosed with cancer at seventeen and injuring my voice at twenty-four. I'm not belittling my marriage or the birth of my son, but these were events of choice. I chose to get married and have a child. I did not choose to get cancer or have an injury that destroyed my voice, nor to have little control over the many actions and events that followed.

"One day, I was saying goodbye to my high school girlfriend, sitting in my small car and looking up as she said goodbye. She noticed a small bump under my chin. She felt it and asked what it was. I told her I didn't think it was anything: it was centered under my chin and didn't look abnormal. She wasn't convinced and had her mom look at it. Her mom said I should see a doctor.

"When I got home, I told Mom. She didn't appear to be overly worried. Nevertheless, a doctor's appointment was made. A few days later, the doctor took a biopsy—needle in and out. Quick, easy, and done. This was 1970, and the biopsy results took a while. After a week, I noticed my family was exceptionally nice to me. Still, I made no connection to the biopsy. At the follow-up doctor's appointment, after another week, I was told I had cancer. I noticed Mom's tears and was later told my family had been informed a week earlier. They waited to tell me while the doctors determined the extent of the cancer. That is why everyone was so kind." Tension filled the room.

"I started down a path of tests, an operation, and medical procedures that were utterly foreign to me. The lymph node under my chin was removed. Many, many needles were inserted into all parts of my body. Bone marrow was taken from my hip, and cuts and needles pierced the top of each foot. I endured scans ninety minutes long. While the scanners went back and forth, I counted the number of holes in the ceiling panel . . . multiple times. I had surgery to remove my spleen and check other abdominal organs, followed by six weeks of radiation. I lost twenty pounds and slept eighteen hours a day. None of this made sense for a seventeen-year-old highly directed kid. It was just a big annoyance. I never felt I was seriously sick or that I might die. Mortality was a foreign idea to me, even though my father had died two years prior, and my grandfather was seriously ill. I never felt abandoned by G-d or that my faith was being tested. I was just a kid dealing with some issues I would get past. I'd go to college and have a great time.

"In the short term, the cancer had only a minor impact." Collective exhale. "It was recommended that I not go to the East Coast for school as planned, having been accepted at Cornell and UMass at Amherst. My high school track career was cut short. I wore a knit beanie to cover the hair I had lost to radiation—a knit beanie on a high school kid in Los Angeles in the middle of June is quite noticeable." Chuckles broke out from those raised in Southern California. "Everyone settled down as I recovered. But in the long term, Hodgkin's has had repeated impacts. A medical deferment from the draft, my thyroid removed, open heart surgery, and a pacemaker can all be traced back to that little lump under my chin. To this day, I never viewed any of this as G-d acting on me or my looking to G-d for context, meaning, or help in curing me or 'giving me the strength' to persevere. Faith versus cancer made no sense to me. Family, friends, and community support made sense and gave me the strength and purpose to deal with my challenges.

"Only leading up to heart surgery did I ever fear I would die. Yet, as the day of the surgery arrived, I had no sense this was the end. I did not need to call for strength through faith. In the next few years, I will have to have heart surgery again. Given my multiple heart issues and my age, I wonder how I will deal with it.

"The second significant event, and the one having a more profound impact on my life, was the injury to my larynx and vocal cords. Three weeks after passing my doctoral exam in politics, a softball game changed my life. I was playing first base when the batter hit a high fly ball in my direction. I chased it while looking up. I knew I'd catch it even as the ball flew further foul. Suddenly, I realized a bleacher was directly in front of me. My first reaction was not to hit my shins on the lowest bench because I knew how much that would hurt. I jumped, landing on the higher seats of the bleacher. With my arms, I protected my head and chest, but I didn't have the strength to stop my momentum. My neck hit the edge of the wooden bleacher board very hard.

"I held my breath and turned to sit on the offending bleacher seat, not knowing what my next breath would bring. Had I damaged my ability to breathe? My next breath would tell—and I was scared. I was able to take a deep breath. The people coming to my aid asked if I was OK. As I responded, my voice started deep, went very high, and then breathy. That was the last I had of a normal voice. The only voice I had was a breathy whisper.

"At first, I thought the loss of voice would be temporary. While annoying, there was a certain humor about only being able to whisper. But as it became clear that the damage was permanent, my view of things changed dramatically. I could not speak to anyone more than a few feet from me. The telephone became my nemesis: I was unable to have comfortable conversations. People could barely hear me. Wives of friends, operators, and service people would hang up on me, thinking I was an obscene caller. And my ability as a single male to meet women became upsetting and disheartening. I was perceived as either ill or just strange. At a minimum, I could not be heard if there was any background noise. One of my worst days was when I went to the Boston Museum. I spoke into a phone set up so I could hear my voice. I was traumatized for days.

"I found that people make their first impression visually and act accordingly. A missing leg—sorry, Peter—being confined to a wheelchair, being blind, and many other limitations are visually noticeable. They immediately create a first impression people use in their interactions. The problem with a speech issue is it's not apparent from a distance. I constantly had to deal with strange looks and reactions as I whispered. Listeners conclude I must be some kind of pervert. Women's reactions were rarely kind and accepting. Instead, they were uncomfortable and dismissive. My personal life became lonely. Luckily, the woman who became my wife gave me a second look. But that was eight years after I lost my voice.

"These two events changed my life forever. I was a graduate student giving lectures and interested in electoral politics. Without a voice, this changed. I couldn't give a lecture and was unable to speak to groups. I couldn't function correctly on the telephone.

Before losing my voice, I'd gone to Boys State and A Presidential Classroom—a national program bringing in students from around the country for a week in Washington, DC. I worked in numerous legislative offices and had almost completed my doctorate. All of these were preparing me for a career in politics. Suddenly, my path changed. The only avenue I saw available was continuing with the doctoral program—to what end, I wasn't sure.

"I did find opportunities—both professional and personal— that carried me forward. Getting selected as a Fellow with the California Assembly enabled me to work in the legislature for eight years and thirty-seven more with the California Department of Education. I married, had children, and served as a temple board member for many years. Nevertheless, every day, there were reminders of how my life trajectory had altered and the risks I had not taken.

"Did faith play any part in how I dealt with these? Not in any overt way. I didn't pray for healing or strength to deal with my challenges. While there were periods of anger and depression, I never stopped striving to succeed. I didn't start going to the temple weekly or reading Jewish texts. However, I did go to the temple for the high holidays and attended seders and other Jewish holiday activities. I always find them comforting and an opportunity for quiet reflection. I got renewed strength from sitting in the temple and knowing that the prayers I recited or sang were the same ones my grandparents and the generations that preceded them had recited. This helped me see what had led to my beliefs and values and how these would affect my children and descendants. This is how I found my place in the greater scheme of things. My voice issues and my cancer got lost as I accepted the responsibility handed down to me over generations.

"Marriage gave me the stability to fully reenter temple life, and I became involved. An early challenge in my marriage created for me a sense of what it meant to be Jewish. The challenge was my wife's celebration of Christmas. I met her at a Jewish singles dance, so I never questioned her commitment to Judaism—that made things easy until she wanted to put up a tree and celebrate

Christmas. That caught me by surprise and was very disturbing. I would remove myself and not participate in the tree or presents. She called me a Grinch. Upsetting."

A low mumble made Sam pause.

"The reason my wife wanted to celebrate Christmas was very profound—at least to me. At the time, she was a single mother with a young child under four years old. She did not have a large community of friends; of these, only a few were Jewish. She wanted to share the holiday with her community, and most importantly, she did not want her child to feel isolated from other kids. Christmas was not a religious holiday for her but rather a secular celebration. She saw no religious conflict. I did. Only after a few years, as our involvement in the local temple expanded and we developed a large support group, did the celebration of Christmas end. Was this a spiritual or other challenge to my Jewishness? I'm not sure, but I was thrilled the first time we didn't put up a Christmas tree.

"Do I believe there is a power, force, or entity greater than myself? This has always been a difficult question for me. When at the temple and praying, who or what am I praying to if not a greater being? How did the world/universe become if there's no greater being? Suppose there is a greater being that I pray to. How could it allow the terrible things that have happened over time, especially to the group I identify with—Jews? The best I've been able to come up with that is consistent with my beliefs and Judaism is G-d is made up of all of us. Striving to make the world better is continuing G-d's work. G-d is the fundamental essence within each of us. And that essence is something that permeates our world. Bad happens when we lose connection with the community and respond to our fears and self-interests. Good happens when we put others ahead of us, or at least try to do so. It's a mixed bag, but this consolidation of the world constitutes a greater force—G-d, if you like.

"I don't believe in miracles, but if I beat Scott at pickleball, I may have to revisit my thoughts about miracles. I'm a good player. I can defeat most people, but Scott is better than anyone I've played before, and he was going easy on us! Scott's reflexes are lightning fast, making watching what he can do on the court fun. He's amazing. Indeed, beating Scott would be a miracle.

"I'm not a person of epiphanies or other moments of realized deep faith. Spirituality for me tends to be in the daily wonders of the world—a beautiful sunrise, the fresh green of the morning golf course as I walk my dog, the smiles of my grandkids, reciting the same prayers that my parents and their parents have recited for thousands of years, the help of friends, the support of my wife— these and other things nourish me spiritually.

"If facing death means we become more aware of our mortality, I guess my thoughts turn to what I've left behind, whether I have done any good, and will my grandchildren remember and honor those who have come before. I don't believe that my spirit, essence, soul, or anything else goes to another life or form or anything else. My body will be cremated, and the ashes returned to the earth. My afterlife will be in the memories of those who think of me, in the lives of those I've touched—whether they remember or not—and in the things I leave behind. For example, I'm trying to organize the family pictures into albums because I know if I don't do it, the memory of those whose photographs and stories I include will be lost. It's why I want my name on a Jewish memorial board in some temple—so I will be remembered. That is my afterlife."

(Applause)

* * *

"Before we take a ten-minute break, some business needs our attention," I said. "Paul told me that some of you have yet to pay for your share of the food. Additionally, a couple of you need to pay your room fees. Please do that before you depart.

"I will be the final presenter."

JOHN'S JOURNEY
Connecting to the Holy

"Thank you for telling us about your spiritual journeys," I began. "I found your stories inspiring. I feel closer to each of you because of what you shared."

"Thank you for the aprons," said Paul. "They're terrific. I'll get a lot of good use out of mine."

"Thank you for suggesting the topic and organizing the gathering," said Bruce. "The talks have been invigorating and sublime."

(Applause)

"I chose to visit the Midway. My senior project as a history major in college was to write about the Battle of Midway. I studied the heroics of the men involved, the strategies of each side, and the battle's implications for the war in the Pacific. On yesterday's tour, I learned the aircraft carrier wasn't commissioned until one week after World War II ended. Nevertheless, being on an aircraft carrier from that era reconnected me to the terror and determination of the men engaged in the struggle. It was a stirring experience for me.

"My presentation is about how my journey unfolded and what I concluded. I'll begin with the religious affiliations of my ancestors. It's an unusual mix. My father's side was Ashkenazi Jews. My great-grandmother, whom I knew, was the last observant family member. She gave me a yarmulke that my parents put away to save for me. I still have it. My grandfather stopped identifying as Jewish when he married a Christian Scientist. He didn't seem to care about religious matters, but his wife did; she was a true believer. My father began his life as a Christian Scientist.

"My mother's background was Norwegian Lutheran. Her mother's devotion to the church led her to give money to restore Trondheim Cathedral's famous rose window. I don't know my Grandfather Pratt's spiritual inclinations or if he had any. He was an official in his local Masonic lodge. When my parents married, they joined the Episcopal Church. My religious heritage is a potpourri of Jewish, Christian Science, and Norwegian Lutheran, with a possible smattering of Masonic lore. These traditions are behind my identity as an Episcopalian. I am a religious mongrel, a blend of diverse beliefs and practices." Chuckles erupted.

"While these diverse beliefs and practices unconsciously influenced my religious development, my parents consciously did. They took the family to church every Sunday. The parish became my second home. I was perplexed, however, by my parents' participation. My father held every parish leadership position possible, yet he never spoke of a spiritual motivation for his involvement. He was a successful businessman who brought those skills to church leadership. He was embarrassed by his Jewish heritage and defensive of his mother's devotion to Christian Science. My mother, in contrast, seemed deeply spiritual without giving it much thought. She didn't speak of her beliefs either.

"Growing up, I was an acolyte and participated in all the essential church services, including celebrity weddings. I received baptism, confirmation, and ordination as a deacon and priest in my home parish. These experiences, from the mundane to the extraordinary, informed my journey.

"My childhood was in Beverly Hills in the 1950s, home to many rich and famous people and a large Jewish population. I sometimes felt like I lived in the promised land. I recall sitting on the front steps of my home, watching the garbage collectors toss my family's discards into the back of the city truck. I wondered why I had a life of privilege while they collected trash. I'd done nothing to deserve my place in society. Why was God treating me so favorably? The stark contrast in living conditions led me to question divine justice. Why does a God of love permit social hierarchies, prejudice, and injustice? As a teenager, I sought answers in the writings of theologians. I was disappointed by their explanation that moral depravity is a consequence of free will. Unfortunately, I haven't found a better answer.

"I admired my father's business success and took too much pride in his achievements. Grandfather Pratt was even more financially successful. Going back another generation, my great-grandfather's sister was the wife of a lawyer who became secretary of state and won a Nobel Peace Prize. These were the men whose achievements I felt the need to replicate. To me, much had been given, and much was expected. The pressure was too much. I was a C student in high school.

"The summer between my junior and senior years—I was sixteen—I went on a cathedral and castle tour of Europe, where an unexpected event shaped my spiritual journey. During our visits to Roman Catholic cathedrals, tourists spoke loudly and took pictures while a priest celebrated the Mass a few feet away. I found this offensive and the church's acceptance of it disheartening. I was pleased Anglican cathedrals had a different approach: visitors not there for the service were asked to leave. In London, my tour group visited Saint Paul's Cathedral. I stepped outside the main doors as a service began. While I waited for the rest of my group, I had an experience I later realized was a vision. I heard a voice I attributed to God telling me I needed to change the church. I was stunned. Was God calling me to be a prophet? The commandment I should change the church seemed ludicrous, but it stimulated my thinking about the church's role in my future. Fantasies of becoming an Episcopal bishop grew, as that was the only way I could envision fulfilling the vision. I kept these things to myself.

"Later, after reading Rudolf Otto's *The Idea of the Holy*, I realized my vision was an expression of the *numinous*, a word Professor Otto used to describe the presence of the Holy. Since the Holy's essence is incomprehensible, Otto used words like *awe, energy, urgency*, and *fascination* to describe the Holy's effect on us. Other effects he noted include fear, trembling, and a sense of humility in the presence of the Supreme Above All—his words. Professor Otto accurately described my vision—I felt all those things—and motivated me to learn more about the Holy.

"In the late fall of my first year of college, I returned to my dorm room dejected. I sat alone, looking out a large window as snow fell. Everything was quiet, Christmas was near, and I felt the love of God lift my downheartedness. Indeed, I felt so much love that I wrote my parents a letter telling them how much I loved and appreciated them. The letter made a strong impression on them because it was out of character for me to do something like that. That afternoon, God's unconditional love became part of my spiritual journey.

"While I was in college, I double-majored in history and philosophy. I was seeking access to the world's wisdom. Spoiler alert: I didn't find it." More chuckles. "I read Emil Brunner, Paul Tillich, Teilhard de Chardin, and other theologians, hoping to gain a deeper insight into my vision. I took a course on world religions to understand the attraction Taoism held for me. The ancient Chinese philosopher Lao Tzu made the observation in the *Tao Te Ching* that one who knows doesn't need to speak and if one is speaking, one doesn't know. I needed to understand what those who do not speak know.

"The next event that influenced my spiritual journey occurred in Los Angeles in the summer of 1966. It was the year after the Watts riots. I was twenty and about to enter my last year of college. I used the summer to explore what it was like to work for a church. A seminarian and I lived at a small, black Episcopal church a few blocks from where the riots stopped. We supervised an education program the congregation offered to the community. The seminarian and I were the only white faces for miles—except for the police officers who monitored the neighborhood from their heavily armed patrol cars. It was quite the opposite of living in Beverly Hills. I came away from the experience convinced people are the same regardless of skin color and that the church can make a difference in people's lives. I decided to proceed with becoming a priest.

"I entered seminary after graduating from college, while many of my classmates went to Vietnam. One friend committed suicide when his induction notice arrived; others died in action. Two of my seminary classmates were recently back from Vietnam, and they were emotionally wounded. One dropped out when the disparity between the battlefield and seminary was too much. These men had faced an evil I did not know. Being around them convinced me evil is more than the absence of good. It is real unto itself."

"I agree," said Andy, lowering his head.

"Between the first and second years of seminary, those aspiring ordination take a quarter of clinical training to try out being ministers. I trained as a hospital chaplain. My supervisor was a Lutheran pastor who demonstrated the practical applications of God's grace. I am grateful for his gift to my development.

"I took an extra year of seminary to participate in a church and society program under the leadership of an ethics professor. I worked on Capitol Hill as an intern in a senator's office. Each Friday afternoon, program participants discussed how we would explain to an imaginary congregation what was happening in government. It was an invigorating and rewarding year. I enjoyed the political work so much that I contemplated dropping out of seminary and continuing as a senate aide. After thinking about it, I decided social action would be part of my ministry.

"I graduated and launched my priestly career in a prominent congregation in San Diego. My boss, Jack Sanford, introduced me to C. G. Jung's perspectives, particularly about religious experience. I learned more about the Holy Spirit from Jack and Jung than I did in seminary.

"I met Robert Johnson during my time in San Diego. He was Jack's close friend. Robert knew more about the soul than any person I've met. I drank in his wisdom but still didn't have an answer to Lao Tzu's riddle about people who know not speaking.

"I also began over ten years of weekly therapy. I was fascinated by dreams and diligently studied mine. During these years, I came to appreciate what I call Rumi's confession, that when he was a young man he was clever and wanted to change the world; later in life he grew wiser and decided to change himself. My focus changed from institutional reform to healing, beginning with my own.

"In my late twenties, I became the rector of the Episcopal church in Monrovia, where Bruce was baptized many years before. I loved my work and the people, so I was shocked when, after only three years, a series of dreams indicated I should leave the parish ministry and become a therapist. I resisted mightily. The parish I headed supported my leadership, which told me moving to a different congregation wouldn't satisfy whatever was fermenting in me. I was married with three young daughters. Leaving a favorable situation for the unknown was terrifying.

"Nevertheless, I resigned. Parishioners told me my decision was foolish; others felt abandoned. Recently, I came across a spiritual teaching that said walking the spiritual path requires continually stepping into the unknown. That is what I did without knowing why. I just knew I had to do it.

"I returned to graduate school, obtained a master's degree in psychology, and became a licensed marriage, family, and child therapist. The change was the correct decision, but it cost me my marriage and financial future. Most of all, I regret the undeserved suffering it inflicted on my children.

"A few years later, I met James Hubbell, the famous San Diego artist. Jim told me you don't have to know where you are going, but you do have to set a direction toward something, hoping it is big enough to last your whole life, even after. My direction was to seek a connection with the Holy. *Adhyatma vikasa* is Sanskrit for becoming aware of the divine within and beyond oneself. It comforts me to know the spiritual masters of India, dating back three or four thousand years, chose the same direction I have.

"The next major event that affected my spiritual journey was when I heard Bill Moyers interview Joseph Campbell. That series of talks about mythology spoke to me profoundly. When I was in seminary, one of my theology professors said if Christianity wasn't grounded in history, he would no longer be a believer.

That comment stuck with me. After studying Campbell and Jung, I didn't need Christianity or the Bible's stories to be based on historical facts, though many are. I consider the significant religious stories to be myths. Myths open us to the transcendent mystery that underlies all things. Contrary to my theology professor's beliefs, death and resurrection don't have to be historically grounded to be true.

"This insight enabled me to step away from Christian orthodoxy into the mainstream of mysticism, where I feel more comfortable. I value faith over belief and regard reality as more than sensual impressions and conclusions. Indeed, an invisible dimension supports the visible one. Albert Einstein observed, 'Everyone who is seriously engaged in the pursuit of science becomes convinced that the laws of nature manifest the existence of a spirit vastly superior to that of men, and one in the face of which we with our modest powers must feel humble.'[9] William James, the famous twentieth-century psychologist who studied a variety of religious experiences, agreed with Einstein. James wrote that some people know an objective presence is with them, that an invisible and divine reality exists. James was describing people like me. The awareness of a reality greater than my ego has always been part of my experience. This Other has been my lifelong companion. Some of you shared you have the same awareness.

"Is there life after death? I suspect so, in some shape or form. There is anecdotal evidence that such a reality exists, even when our rational minds say otherwise. I'll share some anecdotal stories of my own.

"I recall being in the pulpit in Monrovia on All Saints' Day. I don't recall what I said, but I remember being startled by an uproar in the rafters caused by the spirits of deceased parishioners. Their presence came to mind when Richard spoke of the presence he felt on his visit to the Midway. I had no idea who the individual spirits were, but it was a remarkable and joyful moment.

"In my work as a therapist, I heard clients describe visitations from the deceased. Several clients told me dying loved ones

9. Jammer, *Einstein and Religion*, 93.

reported seeing deceased family members coming 'to take them home.'

"I've read Native Americans value the guidance of their ancestors. Shamans leave their bodies to travel to the spirit realm, where they speak directly with the deceased.

"These accounts don't prove the existence of life after death. Still, similar reports from different cultures suggest the possibility. If there is life after death, I'm convinced God doesn't give a theology exam to be with him when we die. What we believe doesn't matter. By grace, everyone enters the fullness of God's love.

"The most persuasive declaration of an afterlife I know comes from a woman's dream. In the 1950s, the woman was in a Los Angeles hospital dying. A close friend visited her often, and the woman recounted the twists and turns of her journey to him. She'd been sleeping when a doctor entered her room to see how she was doing. She woke up and told the doctor the dream she just had. After reporting the dream, she asked the doctor to relay it to her friend. The woman died shortly after sharing this dream:

> There is a candle burning in front of a mirror. The candle and flame are reflected in the mirror. A hand from above appears and snuffs out the flame. After a few moments, the candle in the mirror relights.

"This dream brightens my spirit. Something deep inside me rejoices every time I recall it. Not all of life is rational. Indeed, I believe many of the best parts of life, like love, grace, creativity, beauty, and God reaching out to us in dreams, are not. Nevertheless, they can be as insightful and trustworthy as logical depictions of reality.

"Looking back, the Holy Other pushed my spiritual journey forward, even when I wasn't aware of it. I struggled with divine justice and the presence of evil in its rawness. A vision influenced me to become a priest. I have felt the unconditional love of God. Mentors taught me about grace, Jung and dreams, the workings of the soul, and the significance of mythology. I found theological comfort in the camp of the mystics. The more my ego directed my life, the less fulfilled I was. When I allowed the Holy Spirit to direct me, good things happened. I discovered I am not a prophet, bishop, or institutional reformer; I do better as a healer and one who seeks God within and beyond myself.

"One constant, underlying focus of my journey has been Lao Tzu's observation that 'He who knows does not speak, and he who speaks does not know.' I've concluded that since God's mystery transcends all thinking, direct experiences of the Holy are indescribable. Mine certainly was. Some things the mind can know but not articulate."

(Applause)

* * *

"Thank you. It's time to take a snack break," I said. "Paul, what have you prepared?

"Triple chocolate tiramisu. I want to thank Jim for the help he's given me. He made it possible to have the meals and snacks ready on time, and he is fun to work with." Standing ovation for Jim. "I also want to thank the clean-up crews. You did a splendid job of having everything ready when I needed it. Well done!" More applause.

"Let's eat. We'll say our goodbyes in the morning," I said.

DEPARTING

"Paul, the spinach and mushroom quiches you prepared with a side of fresh fruit were outstanding," I said. "Everyone will be heading home with a full belly. One more round of applause for our excellent cooks: Paul and Jim." Standing ovation.

"Let's hear it for Hal for leading us in our annual sing-along." More applause.

"I liked the songs you added this year," said Lawrence. "Thanks for doing that."

"Lawrence, your strong voice on key helped those who don't have your vocal gifts. That was a valuable contribution to the sing-along," said Hal, smiling.

"One final piece of business," I said. "Thank you for settling your accounts before leaving. Your cooperation has significantly lightened my load.

"Robert will be our host for next year's gathering. He will be in touch to discuss the details of our next meeting, including the date, location, and theme. With Robert's creativity and passion, I'm sure it will be a memorable event. I'm already looking forward to it and hope you are too!

"Once again, I am grateful for your active participation and invaluable contributions. Each of you played a crucial role in making this year's gathering exceptional. Your efforts are truly appreciated.

"As you begin your journey home this Memorial Day weekend, please take a moment to remember and honor those who made the ultimate sacrifice for us. Travel safely, and I look forward to seeing you next year."

THE END

ABOUT JOHN PRATT BINGHAM

John was born and raised in California. He attended Willamette University and the Virginia Theological Seminary. His time in seminary was marked by a unique experience—a year-long internship in the office of Senator Philip Hart, Michigan.

As a parish priest, John was an associate of the Reverend John A. Sanford at Saint Paul's, San Diego, and rector of Saint Luke's, Monrovia, California.

John's path turned when a series of dreams persuaded him to leave the parish ministry. He then embarked on a new journey, training at the C. G. Jung Institute of Los Angeles and earning his master's degree in psychology from Antioch University.

John began his private practice as a marriage and family therapist in 1980. He became executive director of the Samaritan Counseling Center of Greater Sacramento in 1994. He was named a Sacramento Hero in Healthcare shortly after.

Since his retirement in 2013, John has been enjoying his time in San Diego, where he lives close to his five children and nine grandchildren. He spends his days writing, playing euchre, and perfecting his pickleball game.

OTHER PUBLICATIONS

God and Dreams: Is There a Connection?
(Resource Publications, Eugene, Oregon, 2010)
www.wipfandstock.com

Hangtown
(Binghambooks, San Diego, California, 2015)
www.binghambooks.com

Hangtown: Secrets & Schemes
(Binghambooks, San Diego, California, 2018)
www.binghambooks.com

Hangtown: The Dark Night
(Binghambooks, San Diego, California, 2021)
www.binghambooks.com

Inner Treasure: Reflections on Teachings of Jesus
(Dove Publications, Pecos, New Mexico, 1989)
www.amazon.com

CONNECT WITH JOHN

Website: www.binghambooks.com
Facebook: binghambooks

Please consider reviewing *Buddies Share Their Spiritual Journeys* and submit it to your favorite book site. Others will benefit from your appraisal. Most reviews are a sentence or two, though longer contributions are particularly valued. Thank you.

BIBLIOGRAPHY

Alcoholics Anonymous: The Story of How Many Thousands of Men and Women Have Recovered from Alcoholism. 4th ed. New York: Alcoholics Anonymous World Services, 2001. https://www.aa.org/the-big-book.

Hobe, Laura. *Try God.* New York: Doubleday, 1977.

Jammer, Max. *Einstein and Religion: Physics and Theology.* Princeton: Princeton University Press, 1999.

Kurtz, Ernest, and Katherine Ketchem. *The Spirituality of Imperfection: Storytelling and the Search for Meaning.* New York: Bantam, 1992.

The Standing Liturgical Commission. *Enriching Our Worship 1: Morning and Evening Prayer, the Great Litany, the Holy Eucharist.* New York: Church, 1998. https://www.churchpublishing.org/siteassets/pdf/enriching-our-worship-1/enrichingourworship1.pdf.